Information Security: A Legal, Business, and Technical Handbook

Kimberly Kiefer
Stephen Wu
Ben Wilson
Randy Sabett

Section of Science & Technology Law

Defending Liberty
Pursuing Justice

Cover design by ABA Publishing.

The materials contained herein represent the opinions and views of the authors and editors, and should not be construed to be the action of either the American Bar Association or the Section of Science and Technology unless adopted pursuant to the bylaws of the Association.

Nothing contained in this book is to be considered as the rendering of legal advice for specific cases, and readers are responsible for obtaining such advice from their own legal counsel. This book and any forms and agreements herein are intended for educational and informational purposes only.

Printed in the United States of America.

08 07 06 05 04 5 4 3 2 1

Library of Congress Cataloging-in-Publication Data

Information security : a legal, business, and technical handbook / Kimberly Kiefer, editor.
　　p. cm.
　　ISBN 1-59031-300-3
　　1. Computer security—Law and legislation—United States. 2. Data protection—Law and legislation—United States. 3. Computer security—United States. 4. Data protection—United States. I. Kiefer, Kimberly, 1970-

KF390.5.C6I54 2004
342.7308'58—dc22   2003023497

Discounts are available for books ordered in bulk. Special consideration is given to state bars, CLE programs, and other bar-related organizations. Inquire at Book Publishing, ABA Publishing, American Bar Association, 750 North Lake Shore Drive, Chicago, Illinois 60611.

www.ababooks.org

CONTENTS

FOREWORD

The Information Security Committee (ISC) of the American Bar Association Section of Science and Technology Law has developed this book to inform directors, management, other business personnel, and the legal professionals who assist them concerning issues related to information security and law. It has also been designed to help lawyers counsel their clients who maintain electronic records and data used in their business. Some of these records may include confidential information, trade secrets, or information that is considered private, especially in regulated industries such as financial services and health care. Further, this book assists technical personnel who want a basic understanding of information security threats and legal issues related to them.

More specifically, this book provides critical information to lawyers in their roles as advisors on the law in minimizing liability (civil and criminal); contract drafters, reviewers, and counselors concerning the development and implementation of corporate policies; team members responding to security incidents and disasters; advisors in the product and service development process; and counselors participating in the risk management process. The book is equally useful to directors, trustees, and senior managers who have a fiduciary obligation to an organization to exercise due care in conducting its affairs. Given the critical importance of information and information systems to many organizations, attention to protecting against information security attacks becomes an extension of this duty of care. Thus, this book provides guidance to, and information about the role of, directors, trustees, and managers in implementing information security policy and practices.

This book explains what information security is and why your organization should be concerned about it. More specifically, we hope it familiarizes you with:

- the concept of "information security";
- the importance of information security awareness to an organization's business;
- the types of information security faced by an organization;
- federal and state laws and regulations related to information security;
- potential liability that can result from an organization's information systems;
- steps to take in responding to security incidents;
- information security risk management considerations and strategies; and
- safeguards and practices to minimize risks to an organization's information systems.

The book also seeks to provide a wide breadth of coverage, as opposed to in-depth coverage of specific issues. Accordingly, the reader may need to consult other resources for more details about specific issues. It is important to note that this book addresses information security and the law from the domestic perspective and does not address foreign laws, regulations, and industry practices that may, and often do, play a significant role in an organization's information security risk assessment and liability determination. For international aspects of computer crime, *see* http://www.cybercrime.gov/intl.html and http://www.cybercrimes.net/International/International.html. For European data protection laws, *see* http://europa.eu.int/comm/internal_market/en/dataprot/law/impl.htm.

CONTRIBUTORS*

Joseph Alhadeff	Oracle Corporation	Washington, D.C.
Lee Begeja	AT&T Research	
Rebecca Bradley	Whyte Hirschboeck Dudek	Milwaukee, Wis.
Pat Cain	The Cooper-Cain Group	Cambridge, Mass.
Denley Chew	Federal Reserve Bank of New York	New York, N.Y.
Kathryn Coburn	WellPoint Health	Woodland Hills, Cal.
Eric Drogin, J.D., Ph.D.	Franklin Pierce Law Center	Concord, N.H.
Emily Freeman	AIG	San Francisco, Cal.
Emily Frye	George Mason University	Washington, D.C.
Mike Hines	Institute of Internal Auditors	Altamonte Springs, Fla.
Rick Hornbeck	Hornbeck Consulting	Los Angeles, Cal.
Randolph Kahn	Kahn Consulting, Inc.	Highland Park, Ill.
Eleanor Kellett	SCANA Corporation	Columbia, S.C.
Kimberly Kiefer	U.S. Department of Justice	Washington, D.C.
Mary Kirwan	Kasten Chase Applied Research	Toronto, Canada
Jeff Klaben	Applied Materials, Inc.	Santa Clara, Cal.
Mike Jerbic	Trusted Systems Consulting Group	Cupertino, Cal.
Charles Merrill	McCarter & English, LLP	Newark, N.J.
John Messing	Law-on-Line, Inc.	Tucson, Ariz.
Timothy Nagle	TRW Systems & Information Technology	Fairfax, Va.

* The views expressed herein are those of the authors and do not necessarily reflect the views of any of their current or former clients, or their respective current or former employers, including government agencies, such as the Department of Justice and the Department of Treasury.

Bruce Nearon	J.H. Cohn	Roseland, N.J.
Tim Rosenberg	George Washington Solutions	Philadelphia, Pa.
Ira Rubenstein	Microsoft Corporation	Redmond, Wash.
Brian Peretti	Treasury Department	Washington, D.C.
Randy Sabett	Cooley Godward LLP	Reston, Va.
Gib Sorebo	Unisys	McLean, Va.
Jon Stanley	Jon C. Stanley PA, Inc.	Cape Elizabeth, Me.
Alice Sturgeon	SPYRUS	Ottawa, Ontario
David Sweigert	State of Ohio	Columbus, Ohio
Steve Teppler	TimeCertain, LLC	Sarasota, Fla.
Jody Westby	The Work-IT Group	McLean, Va.
Barbara Wellbery	Morrison & Foerster LLP	Washington, D.C.
Cynthia Wickstrom	Orrick, Herrington & Sutcliffe LLP	Menlo Park, Cal.
Eugene Williams	SPARTA, Inc.	Huntsville, Ala.
Ben Wilson	Xcera Consulting, Inc.	Salt Lake City, Utah
Karen Woo	Self-employed	Kuala Lumpur, Malaysia
Joel Wuesthoff	FTI Consulting, Inc.	Los Angeles, Cal.
Miriam Wugmeister	Morrison & Foerster LLP	New York, N.Y.
Stephen Wu	InfoSec Law Group, PC	Mountain View, Cal.

ACKNOWLEDGMENTS

The ISC acknowledges the kindness of the National Automated Clearing House Association, which gave the ABA and ISC permission to reprint and adapt Chapter 4 of its publication *Risk Management for Consumer Internet Payments* (2002). The information from that publication, as adapted, appears in Chapter 5 and Appendix B of this book.

CHAPTER ❖ 1

Introduction

In early February 2000, the Web sites of Yahoo!, eBay, Amazon.com, Excite, E*Trade, and CNN.com began to receive a flood of electronic communications, essentially requests for attention. In a coordinated attack making use of thousands of computers located throughout the Internet, attackers overwhelmed these companies' systems, squeezing out legitimate users and forcing shutdown of their Web sites.

In that same year, three separate hackers attacked the computer systems of the online merchants Creditcards.com, CD Universe, and Egghead.com.[1] The attackers broke into their systems and located the data files that contained credit card numbers. The hackers then made copies and attempted to use this information to extort money from the merchants. In two cases, the attackers posted the stolen credit card numbers on Web sites that allowed anyone who visited the site to obtain the credit card information to perform unauthorized transactions.

In July 2002, an admissions officer at Princeton University used Social Security numbers from Princeton applicants to gain unauthorized access to information intended for applicants of Yale University.

---

1. CNN.com, *Hacker steals huge credit card database* (Dec. 13, 2000), at http://www.cnn.com/2000/TECH/computing/12/13/credit.cards.com. hacked/index.html; USA TODAY, *Hacker posts stolen credit card numbers* (Jan. 10, 2000), at http://www.usatoday.com/life/cyber/tech/cth098.htm; Lori Enos, *Credit Cards Safe Despite Hack, Egghead Says* (Jan. 8, 2001), at http://www.ecommercetimes.com/perl/story/6541.html.

Yale had hired an undergraduate student to construct the admissions Web site used by its applicants, and the student had chosen Social Security numbers as the device by which applicants would authenticate themselves to the site. The Princeton admissions officer used this technique to gain access to the site and obtain admission information without obtaining permission from either Yale or the applicant. The incident was investigated to determine if the admissions officer had violated any laws in gaining access, and both universities had some embarrassing questions to answer.

What do these incidents have in common? They all threaten "information security." In the past decade, information technology has become commonplace. Technology used by scientists and hobbyists 10 years ago is now enmeshed with our everyday lives. More than half of U.S. households have some kind of Internet access. Many households use this access to shop online. We have moved into the information age, in which the gathering, development, use, and distribution of information in electronic form dominates economic activity, and wealth is tied up in electronic information.

With the increase in economic wealth arising from information, however, come increasing threats. Some threats are natural; others are man-made. Threats to information systems include:

- Computer viruses, worms, and other malicious software code;
- Intrusions and other unauthorized access for purposes of vandalism, fraud, theft of intellectual property, or thrill-seeking;
- Denial-of-service attacks, like the ones described above that struck Yahoo, eBay, and Amazon;
- Terrorism or other attacks against physical facilities that contain information and information systems; and
- Fires, floods, earthquakes, and hurricanes that strike communications transmission systems of physical facilities containing data and systems.

I. Why Is Information Security Important?

The economies of the United States and much of the developed world have transitioned from the manufacturing practices of the Industrial Age to the knowledge-based practices that mark the Information Age. A key development is the widespread use of computer hardware and software, computer networks, and the global computer network, the Internet, to compile, communicate, and make use of electronic records. The amount of information created, transferred, and stored electronically has grown as these technologies have become more commonplace. Organizations use this information to increase efficiency. Both businesses and individuals conduct business electronically and maintain records in electronic formats. As a result, they consider their electronic information to be critical assets. Word-processing files, spreadsheets, and e-mails containing trade secrets, information subject to confidentiality agreements, and attorney-client communications have become the life blood of day-to-day business. In short, information itself has become the basis of value and wealth.

The shift from paper to electronic information creates great business efficiencies. Electronic business permits people to conduct business faster, cheaper, more reliably, and with greater capabilities and satisfaction than ever before. At the same time, as information becomes increasingly valuable, it becomes a greater target for theft, fraud, and attack. Even inadvertent or accidental events can damage information systems and result in the loss or corruption of information. Consequently, the critical nature of information means that its protection from man-made and natural threats must be a high priority. In addition, information systems and their use pose significant risks of liability and harm to an organization's reputation. Simply put, the stakes are higher than ever before for the protection of information and information systems.

Historically, people could minimize information misappropriation or misuse simply by restricting physical access to the paper documents. Limiting physical access provided a fairly strong assurance that neither the substance nor the appearance of the documents would be manipulated.

With electronic records, however, many people may have access to information in many different ways. Physical location is less important as computer networks, remote access, and "telecommuting" extend the ability to access information. On the other hand, wrongdoers have more chances to exploit system weaknesses.

With information having increasing value, the low costs and availability of tools that can be used to infiltrate computer systems, and the increasing interconnections between systems, wrongdoers have the means, motive, and opportunity to attack information systems. Moreover, the evidence supports this conclusion. Information system attacks are increasing in frequency and magnitude.[2] Recovering from attacks and preventing future attacks are costing businesses real dollars.

II. What Is "Information Security"?

The term "information security" is an umbrella concept. In its broadest sense, the term refers to the protection of information "assets." Information assets, of course, include not only the information itself, but also computer software, hardware, networks, and the infrastructure supporting information systems.

Information may reside on disk drives, physical media, or transient memory and may constitute intellectual property or confidential information. Information systems compile, utilize, communicate, and store information. Information systems consist of hardware, such as computer servers, networks, desktop and laptop computers, personal digital assistants, pagers, and cellular phones, as well as software, such as operating systems and applications. In a broader sense, the infrastructure supporting data centers and computer systems (i.e., electricity, water, and telecommunications services, as well as heating, ventilation, and air-conditioning systems) is also an information asset.

"Information security" is an umbrella term because it encompasses a large number of disciplines. Some examples include:

- *Security Management Practices*: Actions of management to protect an organization's information assets by developing and implementing security policies and procedures, classifying and

---

2. On April 7, 2002, the Computer Security Institute and the Federal Bureau of Investigation jointly released their seventh annual Computer Crime and Security Survey. The survey results "confirm that the threat from computer crime and other information security breaches continues unabated and that the financial toll is mounting." CSI Press Release, April 7, 2002, at http://www.gocsi.com/press/20020407.html.

Based on responses from 503 computer security practitioners in major U.S. corporations, government agencies, financial institutions, medical institutions, and universities, this year's survey shows other disturbing trends: In 1997, the total annual reported losses were $100,119,555. In five years, that number increased 455%, to $455,848,000. http://www.fbi.gov/congress/congress02/rondick050802.htm.

determining the value of information assets, analyzing and managing risk, auditing, and business continuity and disaster recovery.

- *Physical Security*: Protecting physical facilities and infrastructure from intrusion, theft, tampering, vandalism, unauthorized access, accidents, and natural disasters.

- *Personnel Security*: Providing assurances that personnel used by an organization (employees and contractors) are competent, adequately trained, trustworthy, and managed appropriately.

- *Computer Security*: Protecting information within an information system, including securing the operating system, applications, and access to workstations.[3]

- *"Logical" or Network Security*: Protecting information as it is transmitted from system to system using computer networks and securing those networks from intrusion and unauthorized access.[4]

- *Telecommunications Security*: Protecting information and prevention from unauthorized access to telecommunications systems other than computer networks, such as phone systems, voice-mail systems, facsimile machines, pagers, broadcasting systems, and videoconferencing systems.

- *Operations Security*: Using procedures and systems to ensure that an organization's systems operate correctly and that its operations continue without interruption. This discipline also includes designing an organization's operations to deter, detect, and recover from incidents of theft, tampering, vandalism, fraud, and unauthorized access. Finally, it includes maintaining electronic records and logs that support an organization's business, facilitate investigations of the organization's security, and provide accountability.

Another aspect of information security is the protection of information and information systems by providing critical security goals, features, or capabilities, known in technical circles as "security services." Confidentiality, integrity, and availability are the three corner-

---

3. *See* WARWICK FORD & MICHAEL BAUM, SECURE ELECTRONIC COMMERCE 94 (2001).
4. *See id.*

Table 1-1
Principal Security Capabilities

Principal Security Capabilities	Definitions
Confidentiality	The ability to protect information against intentional or accidental unauthorized disclosure.
Integrity	The ability to protect information against unauthorized and either accidental or intentional corruption, tampering, or other alteration; this capability includes safeguarding the accuracy and completeness of information.
Availability	Providing assurances that information and systems can be reliably and promptly accessed and used when they are needed.
Authentication	Assuring that a person, organization, or device is who or what he, she, or it purports to be.
Authorization	Administering, monitoring, and controlling the security system. Authorization may include the granting of specific privileges to one or more users.
Access Control	The ability to restrict access to information to authorized personnel, organizations, or devices.
Accountability	The ability to identify the person or organization that performed, or is responsible for, the actions affecting information.
Assurance	Confidence that the system works to its specification without defect or vulnerability.
Nonrepudiation	The capability of providing evidence that can be used against a person or organization attempting falsely to deny having sent or received a specific communication or having engaged in a specific transaction.

stone goals that every information security program attempts to achieve, but others also play a role in information security programs. Table 1-1 summarizes the principal security capabilities commonly listed in information security literature.

Finally, another aspect of information security is the risk management process that security professionals undertake when protecting information and information systems. The process includes identifying the universe of possible threats to information assets, determining whether the information assets are vulnerable to these threats, and implementing appropriate and cost-effective safeguards to address such threats. A threat is the possibility that any man-made, accidental, or natural event may damage information or information systems. Vulnerabilities exist when there is an absence of or weakness in a safeguard to address a threat.

Risk analysis is the process of determining the threats to information assets and their degree of vulnerability. The risk management process includes the risk analysis process but also includes the process of minimizing, accepting, or shifting risk. Anything done to increase security safeguards (equipment, software, policies, and procedures) will reduce risks posed by threats, but will have both monetary and non-monetary costs. The likelihood, magnitude, and possibility of recurrence of the harm must be weighed against the effectiveness and cost of a safeguard meant to address it. In weighing the need for a safeguard, it is important to determine the value of the information assets being protected and degree to which these assets are critical to the continued existence of the organization. One way to measure the importance of information assets is to ask what the cost and impact would be if their security were compromised.

In some instances, an organization will find it cost-effective to implement a safeguard. In other instances, such as where the information assets threatened are not critical or the harm is unlikely or insignificant, the organization may accept a certain level of risk. However, as we have seen from the events on September 11, 2001, even the most unlikely scenario may occur. In such cases, the organization may wish to address these risks by shifting the risk through insurance or indemnities imposed on other parties to pay for the organization's losses.

Having defined the broad concept of information security, it is helpful here to clarify its scope and distinguish it from other concepts.

First, information security involves more than simply protecting against intrusions and thefts by "hackers" (unauthorized third parties). It is also broader than criminal activity affecting information and information systems, such as "cybercrime" (using the Internet or computers for criminal purposes) and economic espionage.

Information security is different from "information privacy," although the two concepts often overlap. Information privacy is the protection of a person's nonpublic personal information by:

- limiting the amount and kind of personal information gathered and stored;
- notifying the person of the ways in which his or her information is used or disclosed;
- obtaining the person's consent to such uses and disclosure;
- providing means for a person to review and update his or her own personal information; and/or
- giving the person the ability to hold someone accountable for the failure to afford these protections.

Information privacy also means that a person's private information will be kept secure against loss, theft, and corruption, in addition to unauthorized access, use, or disclosure of such information. One cannot have information privacy without security. Indeed, statutes, regulations,[5] and industry guidelines that address privacy also require organizations to implement security measures to protect personal information. As a result, there is a considerable overlap between privacy compliance and security obligations. Nonetheless, privacy is broader than security. For instance, an organization that has implemented security precautions to protect its consumer information and

---

5. For instance, the Health Insurance Portability and Accountability Act requires health plans, health-care clearinghouses, and health-care providers to secure patient health information. 42 U.S.C. § 1320d-2(d); Health Insurance Reform: Security Standards, 45 C.F.R. pts. 160, 162, 164. In addition, the Gramm-Leach-Bliley Act states that "each financial institution has an affirmative continuing obligation to respect the privacy of its customers and to protect the security and confidentiality of those customers' nonpublic personal information." 15 U.S.C. § 6801(a).

communicates this information securely to a third-party marketing company for the purpose of sending advertisements to consumers may violate the privacy rights of those consumers.

III. Anatomy of a Hacking Attack

This section sets forth some basic concepts regarding a hacking attack against a computer system. While such attacks may take various forms, and all are unique in their own way, this section will provide basic concepts so that the reader may understand how such attacks occur.

Before conducting an attack, an intruder first conducts a reconnaissance mission to determine the makeup of the computer system. The hacker first identifies the potential target. Through the use of various computer programs, the hacker will test the subject computer system to discover vulnerabilities and determine various avenues to access the system without obtaining authorization from its owner or operator. While damage can occur to the system in this stage, such damage is not the primary objective of the hacker; the goal is to determine system strengths and weaknesses.

While exploring the system, the hacker may create a "back door." A back door is a piece of computer code that permits circumvention of the computer's security features. The hacker may also install other types of code in the system that will permit him to use the system to launch a coordinated attack with other systems against third parties— for example, the attacks against eBay, Yahoo, and CNN described on page 1.

After thoroughly reviewing the system's vulnerabilities, the hacker can then get down to business. With a clear objective in mind and knowledge of what the system can do, the hacker will use the system to achieve his objective. This may include either active (e.g., deletion of files) or passive (e.g., commanding the system to perform tasks that it was not designed to do, such as attacking other systems, or slowing down the system to cause interruption to the daily system work flow) system damage. In either event, there is a loss to the organization because of a decrease in productivity, since the system's resources cannot be used in the most efficient manner.

The hacker may also insert additional code into the system that, while not effective immediately, can cause damage later on. For example, a hacker can install a virus or worm that will become effective at a certain time or date in the future. While some of these programs may just cause the system to slow, they can also be designed to self-replicate and spread to any computer connected to the compromised computer.

In some instances, the object of the hacker is not to destroy, but to steal. Here, the hacker uses the identified vulnerabilities to copy sensitive files on the system to the hacker's system or to another system controlled by him. Hackers may target trade secrets, credit card numbers, user identification and passwords, or employee or customer information. In this type of attack, the hacker does not delete or alter the original files, but merely copies what is on the target system.

If such an attack occurs, the damage can be considerable. While it may appear that the damage is not extensive—for example, where the hacker merely copies the files (the system can be fixed by "closing" the back door and upgrading the system's security)—there are other costs. Customers may not wish to deal with an organization that cannot adequately secure the information that the customer has entrusted to it. As a result, there may be both an increase in costs (for security) and a decrease in revenue (customers moving to more secure providers).

In addition, if there is an actual deletion or corruption of data, the financial costs could be even higher. For example, the hacker might obtain the organization's trade secrets and make a copy for himself and then corrupt the remaining trade secrets on the system in such a way as to cause actual damage to the organization. Since many organizations do not question what is on their system, a slight modification to a formula may not be noticed until the product manufacture is complete. Thus, any products produced under the faulty formula will have to be recalled from the distribution chain and destroyed. The organization will have to commit resources to correcting the corrupted data through testing before the manufacturing process can resume.

The organization can also be damaged by having its trade secrets or customer lists fall into the wrong hands. If a hacker provides this information to a competitor, the target company may lose sales without knowing why. While such a practice is highly unethical, some companies may purchase this information to increase their market position.

CHAPTER ❖ 2

Threats to Information Security

The threats to an information system are wide ranging, from the person or organization wishing to commit espionage to the hacker who wishes merely to prove to himself and the hacking community that he can enter the system. However, not all threats are motivated by a desire to do wrong. Natural disasters and true accidents may also compromise an information system. The following list provides a brief description of the various kinds of information security threats that an organization may face.

I. Threats Based on Intentional Conduct

■ *Hacking*: Attacks against computer systems (often on a network), bypassing security mechanisms, or other intentional breaches of computer security.[1] The motivations for hacking attacks vary widely.

■ *Organized crime*: Attacks by members of organized crime organizations engaging in continuing criminal activity, conducted

---

1. *See* TechTarget, Inc., cracker (visited Nov. 14, 2002), at http://searchsecurity.techtarget.com/sDefinition/0,,sid14_gci211852,00.html. Many in the security industry prefer the term "cracking" to "hacking" because the original connotations of "hacking" were positive, and the term referred to the application of clever programming techniques to achieve some elegant solution to a problem or challenge. *See id.*; TechTarget, Inc., hacker (visited Nov. 14, 2002).

through continuing criminal conspiracies, often utilizing corruption and violence.[2] Criminal organizations may have different motivations, including economic espionage, theft, and sabotage.

- *Insider attacks*: Attacks against an organization by its own current or former employees. The motivation of the employee may range from financial gain (theft of trade secrets and other sensitive information for sale) to revenge for perceived wrongs committed against him or her.

- *Attacks by contractors, vendors, service providers, agents, business partners, and other third parties*: Attacks by people that abuse authorized access to an organization's networks and information. In many instances, third parties provide critical services to an organization involving its sensitive information. The misappropriation or misuse of that information could cause the organization considerable damage. These attacks are often motivated by financial gain.

- *State-sponsored espionage*: Spying attacks conducted in order to gain access to sensitive or valuable information for economic, national policy, or military reasons.

- *Industrial espionage*: Spying attacks conducted to gain access to sensitive or valuable information enabling an organization to gain an economic advantage over its competitors.

- *Terrorism and information warfare*: Attacks by terrorists or state actors meant to further political, ideological, economic, or military goals. Some attacks of this kind are in the nature of intelligence gathering, while others attempt to destroy the victim organization's or nation's assets or ability to defend itself.

- *Malicious code*: Software programs that attack, destroy, or modify information on the victim organization's systems. Examples include:

  - *Viruses*: "A virus is a piece of programming code usually disguised as something else that causes some unexpected

---

2. *See* Nathanson Centre for the Study of Organized Crime and Corruption, Nathanson Centre for the Study of Organized Crime and Corruption Mandate (visited Nov. 14, 2002), at http://www.yorku.ca/nathanson/page3mandate.htm.

and usually undesirable event. A virus is often designed so that it is automatically spread to other computer users."[3]

- *Worms*: "A worm is a self-replicating virus that does not alter files but resides in active memory and duplicates itself. Worms use parts of an operating system that are automatic and usually invisible to the user. It is common for worms to be noticed only when their uncontrolled replication consumes system resources, slowing or halting other tasks."[4]

- *Trojan horses*: A "Trojan horse is a program in which malicious or harmful code is contained inside apparently harmless programming or data in such a way that it can get control and do its chosen form of damage."[5]

- *Malicious scripts*: A program embedded in a Web site or some other interactive mechanism that will cause some degree of damage to a system. For instance, some scripts delivered through Web pages can crash a computer or cause multiple pop-up windows to open.

- *Social engineering*: The use of social skills to obtain knowledge about an organization, obtain passwords or PINs, or gain unauthorized access to information or physical locations. This occurs when an attacker convinces an insider to share his password. The attacker then uses the password to impersonate the insider and perform actions that could have been done by the insider.

- *Physical security breaches*: Intrusions into physical locations within an organization's facility or accessing information from media or paper records in an organization's garbage, recycling bins, shredding bins, or other disposal sites ("dumpster diving"). The motivation for these breaches may include reconnaissance or preparation for later attacks, theft of equipment or trade secrets, or vandalism.

---

3. *See* TechTarget, Inc., virus (visited Nov. 14, 2002), at http://searchsecurity.techtarget.com/sDefinition/0,,sid14_gci213306,00.html.
4. *See* TechTarget, Inc., worm (visited Nov. 14, 2002), at http://searchsecurity.techtarget.com/sDefinition/0,,sid14_gci213386,00.html.
5. *See* TechTarget, Inc., Trojan horse (visited Nov. 14, 2002), at http://searchsecurity.techtarget.com/sDefinition/0,,sid14_gci213221,00.html.

- *Obtaining unauthorized access*: This occurs when someone not authorized to use the system obtains legitimate network credentials (e.g., a username and password) and uses them to gain access. An attacker gaining unauthorized access in this way can, among other things, view restricted or confidential information, compromise the integrity of information, or erase crucial information.
- *Eavesdropping*: An attack to intercept and capture information communicated on a network or displayed by a computer. An act of "sniffing," for instance, involves the use of software that can view and capture user names, passwords, e-mail addresses, and other sensitive information that passes through a network. The eavesdropping may not be detected by the victims. Another form of eavesdropping involves the interception of Radio Frequency (RF) signals emanating from computer screens or terminals and using the signals to display the information appearing on such screens or terminals.
- *Denial of service*: A denial-of-service (DOS) attack seeks to prevent legitimate users' access to a system by flooding the system with illegitimate traffic. A more sophisticated version of a DOS attack involves an attacker taking control of hundreds or even thousands of computers and using them to launch a coordinated attack against a target, known as a "distributed denial of service" attack (DDoS).
- *Relay attack*: A relay attack involves an attacker taking control of a chain of computer systems used to channel or "relay" the attack from system to system in order to cover the tracks of the attacker and make tracing the attacker more difficult.
- *Spoofing*: The impersonation of the purported sender of a message or the use of a phony Web site to impersonate an organization having a legitimate Web site.
- *Fraud*: The misuse of information systems to deceive, mislead, falsify, or misappropriate in order to obtain money or property or achieve some improper result. Examples of improper results include vote fraud, changing grades on a school computer, or changing a minor's identification credential for the purpose of making the minor appear older.

- *Software or media piracy*: The use of information systems to make unauthorized copies of software, video, or audio content.
- *The use of unauthorized or illegal content*: The use of information systems to create, manage, distribute, and store unauthorized or illegal content. The information typically consists of pornography, especially child pornography.

II. Threats Based on Accidental, Inadvertent, or Natural Events

- *Bugs and defects*: Hardware and software flaws that cause malfunctions or create vulnerabilities to attack.
- *Human error*: People make mistakes. These mistakes may cause an information system to operate incorrectly or leave an organization vulnerable. Errors include typographical errors, failures to follow security procedures, incompetence, and mistakes in judgment.
- *Accidents*: Various kinds of accidents may affect information systems, including fires, water-pipe breaks, physical damage to computer equipment, the erasure of media by exposure to magnetic fields, and accidental deletion of information.
- *Disruption of infrastructural services*: Outages of water, heating, air conditioning, gas, or electricity; fiber optic cable cuts; phone line breakage; and similar events may prevent the smooth operation of information systems and can render security precautions ineffective.
- *Natural disasters*: Earthquakes, hurricanes, lightning, floods, fires, and the like may harm security measures enacted to protect the organization's information systems.

CHAPTER ❖ 3

Compliance Issues

Government has made it known that security is an important concern. This has been done through the normal process: Lawmakers enact statutes that impose security requirements, and regulations are promulgated to flesh out these requirements. One aspect of these regulations is the requirement that regulated parties seek assurances of information security in the course of negotiating agreements with third parties. This section provides a brief overview of some of the sources of obligations to secure information systems in public and private law.

I. Sources of Statutory and Regulatory Requirements

A. GRAMM-LEACH-BLILEY ACT

In the financial services sector, Title V of the Gramm-Leach-Bliley Act (GLB) addresses protecting the privacy of consumers' nonpublic personal information held by financial institutions. GLB requires financial institutions, among other things, to provide customers with (i) an initial and annual notice that accurately reflects the financial institution's privacy policies and practices, and (ii) an opportunity to prevent their information from being shared with nonaffiliated third parties. In addition to certain privacy requirements, GLB also addresses information security. Section 501(b) of GLB requires regulatory agencies to establish appropriate standards for financial institutions subject to their respective jurisdictions relating to administrative, technical, and physical safeguards protecting nonpublic personal information. The safeguards are specifically designed to:

(i) ensure the security and confidentiality of customer records and information;

(ii) protect against any anticipated threats or hazards to the security or integrity of such records; and

(iii) protect against unauthorized access to or use of such records or information that could result in substantial harm or inconvenience to any customer.[1]

On January 17, 2001, the federal banking agencies released a set of final guidelines to implement section 501(b) (Guidelines).[2] As a general matter, the Guidelines require financial institutions to establish a comprehensive security program to:

(i) identify and assess the risks that may threaten customer information;

(ii) develop a written plan containing policies and procedures to manage and control these risks;

(iii) implement and test the plan; and

(iv) adjust the plan on a continuing basis to account for changes in technology, the sensitivity of customer information, and internal or external threats to information security.[3]

---

1. *Id.* § 501(b).

2. Interagency Guidelines Establishing Standards for Safeguarding Customer Information, 66 Fed. Reg. 8616 (Feb. 1, 2001); 12 C.F.R. pt. 30 (Office of the Comptroller of the Currency), 12 C.F.R. pts. 208, 211, 225, and 263 (Board of Governors of the Federal Reserve System), 12 C.F.R. pts. 308 and 364 (Federal Deposit Insurance Corporation), and 12 C.F.R. pts. 568 and 570 (Office of Thrift Supervision). The Guidelines became effective on July 1, 2001. The National Credit Union Administration and the Commodity Futures Trading Commission have also issued guidelines under the authority granted by GLB.

3. Joint Press Release of the Board of Governors of the Federal Reserve System, the Federal Deposit Insurance Corporation, the Office of the Comptroller of the Currency, and the Office of Thrift Supervision, Agencies Adopt Guidelines for Customer Information Security (Jan. 17, 2001). As a supplement, in December 2002, the Federal Financial Institutions Examination Council issued an "Information Security" IT Examination Handbook, *available at* http://www.ffiec.gov.

The program must be designed to ensure the security and confidentiality of customer information, protect against unanticipated threats or hazards to the security or integrity of such information, and protect against unauthorized access to, or use of, such customer information that could result in substantial harm or inconvenience to any customer. The Guidelines also place specific obligations on the financial institution's board of directors to: (i) approve the security policy and program; and (ii) exercise general oversight over the program. Finally, the Guidelines require financial institutions to oversee third-party service providers with respect to the security of customer information that is maintained or processed on behalf of the institution.

In addition, the Securities and Exchange Commission adopted Regulation S-P: Privacy of Consumer Financial Information to implement the privacy provisions of GLB.[4] Regulation S-P requires organizations subject to the SEC's jurisdiction to adopt policies and procedures that address administrative, technical, and physical safeguards to protect customer information.

The Federal Trade Commission (FTC) has also issued a final rule implementing section 501(b) of GLB (FTC Rule).[5] The FTC Rule is less extensive and comprehensive than the Guidelines, but does require financial institutions subject to FTC jurisdiction to develop and implement a comprehensive security program appropriate to their size and complexity, the nature and scope of their activities, and the sensitivity of any customer information they possess.[6] It is important to note that the FTC has taken a very broad approach to defining "financial institution." Therefore, organizations that may not normally be considered a financial institution, such as a travel agency or a law firm that provides certain services, may fall under the FTC's jurisdiction.[7]

---

4. 17 C.F.R. pt. 248.
5. 16 C.F.R. pt. 314.
6. 16 C.F.R. pt. 314.3(a).
7. Brian J. Peretti & Dennis Dow, *Gramm-Leach-Bliley and the Bankruptcy/ Collection Attorney*, NORTON BANKRUPTCY LAW ADVISER, Feb. 2002.

B. HEALTH INSURANCE PORTABILITY AND ACCOUNTABILITY ACT

The Health Insurance Portability and Accountability Act (HIPAA)[8] broadly addresses various health-care reforms. HIPAA Title II, subtitle F, addresses "administrative simplification" and covers health plans, heath-care clearinghouses that process health-care transactions, and health-care providers. The administrative simplification provisions have several main components. First, entities covered by HIPAA must, if they perform certain standard health-care transactions electronically, use electronic data interchange (EDI) formats and "code sets" adopted by the Department of Health and Human Services (DHHS). Second, DHHS promulgated regulations (Privacy Rule) providing for the protection of the privacy of "individually identifiable health information" created, received or otherwise in the possession of HIPAA-covered entities.[9]

HIPAA also requires DHHS to issue a separate security regulation, which it did in final form on February 20, 2003.[10] HIPAA regulations provide for uniform, comprehensive protection of individually identifiable health information in two separate standards. First, under the Security Standard, all HIPAA-covered entities that maintain or transmit health information electronically must establish and maintain reasonable and appropriate administrative, technical, and physical safeguards to protect this information. Second, under the Electronic Signature Standard, the implementation of which is currently delayed, all HIPAA-covered entities that use electronic signatures in a transaction covered by HIPAA must meet the requirements set forth in the regulations. These requirements state that electronic signatures must have certain capabilities.

C. SARBANES-OXLEY ACT

The Sarbanes-Oxley Act of 2002[11] requires, among other things, that a public company's chief executive officer and chief financial officer

---

8. Health Insurance Portability and Accountability Act of 1996, Pub. L. No. 104-191, 110 Stat. 1936 (1996).
9. 45 C.F.R. pts.160, 164.
10. 63 Fed. Reg. 43,242, 43,268-69.
11. Sarbanes-Oxley Act of 2002, Pub. L. No. 107-204, 116 Stat. 745 (2002).

certify in each annual or quarterly report filed with the SEC that the signing officer has reviewed the report, the report does not contain untrue statements of material facts, and the financial information fairly presents the financial condition of the company. The signing officers are responsible for establishing and maintaining internal controls to ensure that material information is made known to the officers and must report their conclusions about the effectiveness of these controls, based on an evaluation, within 90 days of making the report. They must also disclose to auditors all deficiencies in internal controls and any fraud conducted by management or employees who have a significant role in the company's internal controls. Finally, the signing officers must indicate in the report whether there are significant changes in internal controls or other factors that could affect internal controls after their evaluation, including significant deficiencies and material weaknesses in the controls.[12]

The Act also calls for SEC regulation requiring certain disclosures in public companies' annual reports.[13] Annual reports must contain an internal control report that states the responsibility of management to establish and maintain adequate internal controls and procedures for financial reporting. An internal control report must also contain an assessment of the effectiveness of the company's internal control structure and procedures for financial reporting. An accounting firm that prepares or issues an audit report relating to the assessment must attest to and report on the assessment made by the company's management, consistent with standards established by the Public Company Accounting Oversight Board.

If information security attacks were to occur that resulted in the alteration of records or falsification of financial results, the company could be held liable for making untrue statements of material facts and inaccuracies in financial reports if this is not included in the report. Moreover, a violation could occur if members of management or employees responsible for internal controls over financial systems compromise those controls or commit fraud for the purpose of inflating the company's financial results. Finally, the failure to report compromises in internal controls or corrective actions involving computer systems holding financial records may be a violation.

---

12. 15 U.S.C. § 7241(a).
13. 15 U.S.C. § 7262.

D. GISRA/FISMA

The Government Information Security Reform Act (GISRA)[14] requires federal government agencies to advance information security through assessing the risks they face, reporting their information security status (including security deficiencies), and including security matters in requests for funding.

The Federal Information Security Management Act (FISMA)[15] strengthens existing protections by requiring the Director of the Office of Management and Budget to require federal agencies to identify and provide information security protections commensurate with the risks they face. The controls must address unauthorized use, disclosure, disruption, modification, or destruction of information or information systems. Agencies' management must provide for the security of their systems and develop security plans and procedures to ensure the continuity of their operations.

E. FEDERAL TRADE COMMISSION OVERSIGHT

The Federal Trade Commission (FTC) has played a central role in establishing, developing, and implementing standards and rules regarding the online collection, use, and disclosure of personal information, in part through the issuance of a series of reports recommending and applying certain practice principles.[16] One such practice principle is the security principle, which requires that data must be accurate and secure. To comply with this principle, companies are expected to employ reasonable measures to ensure integrity of data and managerial and technical measures to protect against loss, unauthorized access, destruction, and disclosure of data. The FTC's authority under the Federal Trade Commission Act[17] (FTCA) creates a mechanism to sanction

---

14. Government Information Security Reform Act, *in* National Defense Authorization Act, Fiscal Year 2001, Pub. L. No. 106-398, 114 Stat. 1654, 1654A-266 (2000).
15. H.R. 3844, 107th Cong. (2002). H.R. 3844 was included in H.R. 2458, the E-Government Act of 2002, and signed into law by President George W. Bush on Dec. 17, 2002.
16. FTC's Online Privacy Reports to Congress, *available at* http://www.ftc.gov/privacy/index.html.
17. 15 U.S.C. § 1, et seq.

organizations in which self-regulatory efforts are unsuccessful. In effect, when an organization does not comply with its posted privacy and security statements and policies, the FTC will consider such failure to be an unfair or deceptive trade practice in violation of the FTCA.

The FTC has brought several actions against companies for failing to strictly adhere to their privacy statements.[18] These actions typically involve an organization's disclosure of consumer information to third parties despite assurances that the organization would not disclose the information without the consumer's consent. The first action to address failure to comply with a security statement made in a privacy policy was the *Eli Lilly* case, which involved the unintended disclosure of prescription drug users' personal information.[19]

Eli Lilly is a pharmaceutical company that offered an "e-mail reminder service" designed to tell customers when it was time to take or refill their medication. The reminders were individualized e-mails that did not identify any other subscribers to the service. To announce the termination of the service, however, Eli Lilly sent subscribers an e-mail that included all of the recipients' e-mail addresses within the "To:" line of the message, thereby disclosing to all subscribers the e-mail addresses of all the other subscribers to the service. On Eli Lilly's Web site, the organization had posted a privacy policy containing several statements regarding the privacy and confidentiality of personal information collected through its Web sites, including the assurance that "[o]ur Web sites have security measures in place, including the use of industry standard secure socket layer encryption (SSL), to protect the confidentiality of any of Your Information that you volunteer. . . ."[20]

In its complaint, the FTC stated that this disclosure of personal information "resulted from [Eli Lilly's] failure to maintain or implement internal measures appropriate under the circumstances to protect sensitive consumer information."[21] In particular, the FTC noted that Eli Lilly failed to provide appropriate employee training regarding privacy and security and appropriate oversight and assistance for the employee who sent

---

18. The FTC's enforcement actions against, for example, geocities.com and ToySmart.com are *available at* http://www.ftc.gov/privacy/index.html.
19. *Available at* http://www.ftc.gov/opa/2002/01/elililly.htm.
20. *In re* Eli Lilly & Co., No. 0123214 (F.T.C.) (complaint), *available at* http://www.ftc.gov/os/2002/01/lillycmp.pdf.
21. *Id.*

out the e-mail. Because the FTC found that Eli Lilly made representations that it employed measures appropriate under the circumstances to protect the privacy and confidentiality of consumer information, such failure amounted to an unfair or deceptive act under the FTCA.

As part of the agreement and consent order with the FTC, Eli Lilly was required to establish and maintain an information security program for the protection of personally identifiable information collected from consumers.[22]

The second action to address failure to comply with a security statement made in the privacy policy is the *Microsoft Passport* case, which, unlike *Eli Lilly,* did not involve a security compromise, but similar to *Eli Lilly,* involved the misrepresentation of the level of security used to protect consumer information.[23]

In July 2001, a coalition of consumer groups led by the Electronic Privacy Information Center (EPIC) filed a complaint with the FTC regarding certain representations made by Microsoft in connection with its "Passport" Web services. These services included Passport Single Sign-On (Passport), which allows users to sign in at any participating Web site with a password and user name; Passport Wallet, which collects and stores credit card numbers and billing and shipping information for users; and Kids Passport, which allows parents to create specialized accounts for their children. One year after the complaint was filed by EPIC, the FTC completed its investigation and entered into a settlement with Microsoft.

On the passport.com Web site, Microsoft made several representations regarding the privacy and security of the Passport services, including, among others, the statements that ".NET Passport achieves a high level of Web Security by using technologies and systems designed to prevent unauthorized access to your personal information," " . . . .NET Passport is protected by powerful online security technology . . . ," and "[y]our .NET Passport information is stored on secure .NET Passport servers that are protected in controlled facilities."[24] In

---

22. *In re* Eli Lilly & Co., No. 0123214 (F.T.C.) (agreement containing consent order), *available at* http://www.ftc.gov/os/2002/01/lillyagree.pdf.
23. *Available at* http://www.ftc.gov/opa/2002/08/microsoft.htm.
24. *In re* Microsoft Corp., No. 123240 (F.T.C.) (complaint), *available at* http://www.ftc.gov/os/2002/08/microsoftcmp.pdf.

its complaint, the FTC alleged that Microsoft failed to maintain a high level of online security as represented in these statements by, in particular, failing to document and implement procedures "that were reasonable and appropriate to: (1) prevent possible unauthorized access to the Passport system; (2) detect possible unauthorized access to the Passport system; (3) monitor the Passport system for potential vulnerabilities; and (4) record and retain system information sufficient to perform security audits and investigations."[25] As a result, the representations were false or misleading in violation of the FTCA.

Similar to the settlement in the *Eli Lilly* case, the agreement and consent order requires Microsoft to establish and maintain a comprehensive information security program for the protection of personally identifiable information collected from consumers.[26] Microsoft is also required, however, to undergo an assessment and report on a biannual basis from an independent third-party professional.[27]

The *Eli Lilly* and *Microsoft* cases may have broad application to all organizations that have a posted privacy notice encompassing some type of security statement and do not adequately protect consumer information from unauthorized access, use, and disclosure and/or properly train their employees in privacy and security.

F. CHILDREN'S ONLINE PRIVACY PROTECTION ACT

The Children's Online Privacy Protection Act of 1998 (COPPA),[28] which became effective April 21, 2000, prohibits Web sites from collecting, using, or disclosing personal information from children under 13 years of age without verifiable parental consent. In the area of security, COPPA requires the FTC to promulgate regulations that require Web site operators to "establish and maintain reasonable procedures to protect the confidentiality, security, and integrity of personal information collected from children."[29]

---

25. *Id.*
26. *In re* Microsoft Corp., No. 123240 (F.T.C.) (agreement containing consent order), *available at* http://www.ftc.gov/os/2002/08/microsoftagree.pdf.
27. *Id.*
28. 15 U.S.C. §§ 6501-6506.
29. 15 U.S.C. § 6502. *See* 16 C.F.R. pt. 312 for the FTC's implementing regulations. *See* http://ftc.gov/opa/2002/04/coppaanniv.htm for the latest FTC initiatives designed to enhance compliance with the act.

G. FEDERAL PRIVACY ACT

The Privacy Act of 1974[30] is an omnibus "code of fair information practices," which seeks to regulate the collection, protection, use, and diffusion of personal information by federal government agencies. Under the act, government agencies that maintain a system of individual records are required to, among other things, "establish appropriate administrative, technical and physical safeguards to insure the security and confidentiality of records and to protect against any anticipated threats or hazards to their security or integrity which could result in substantial harm, embarrassment, inconvenience, or unfairness to any individual on whom information is maintained."[31]

The Privacy Act provides for civil remedies to those individuals who request that federal agencies make changes to correct information within any system of records used by an agency to maintain information on an individual. Essentially, the law directs that information maintained in a system of records must be protected from unauthorized disclosure, used for stated purposes, and maintained in accurate form.

H. STATE LAWS

Some state laws create reporting requirements for information security breaches. For example, California law now requires state agencies and any businesses conducting business in California that possess personal information to disclose any breach of security in their information systems. State agencies and businesses must notify any individuals whose unencrypted personal information was acquired by an unauthorized person.[32] Under Minnesota law, persons who have reason to believe a computer crime has occurred have an obligation to report the crime to prosecutors.[33] Utah law contains a similar provision.[34] In light of laws requiring the reporting of computer crimes, organizations that have been victimized by such crimes may have an obligation to report them.

---

30. 5 U.S.C. § 552a.
31. 5 U.S.C. § 552a (e)(10).
32. CAL. CIV. CODE §§ 1798.29(a), 1798.82(a).
33. MINN. STAT. § 609.8911.
34. UTAH CODE ANN. § 76-6-705.

In these states, declining to take action is not an option.[35]

Companies that are victims of information security breaches may also face liability under a state's consumer protection statute, as illustrated in the case *In the Matter of Ziff Davis Media Inc.*[36] In this case, the Attorneys General from the states of New York, California, and Vermont brought an action under their respective state unfair and deceptive trade practices statutes against a company for failing to take adequate security measures to protect consumer data.

Ziff-Davis Media, Inc., a New York-based company, is a multimedia content company whose primary business is publishing.[37] In November 2001, Ziff-Davis ran a promotion on its Web site for one of its publications, the *Electronic Gaming Monthly*, and received several thousand orders for the magazine. Inadequate security controls resulted in the computer file containing approximately 12,000 customer orders, including personal data and credit card numbers, to be exposed to anyone surfing the Internet.[38] As a result of the data exposure, at least five consumers experienced fraudulent credit card charges made on their accounts.[39] Notably, once Ziff-Davis was made aware of the breach (three days after it ran the promotion), it immediately took a number of curative steps, including deleting the data file from the server, rewriting the applicable code, and notifying affected consumers of the breach.

In its online privacy policy, Ziff-Davis made several representations concerning the privacy and security of personal information collected from consumers, including the following:

> *Security.* We use reasonable precautions to keep the personal information you disclose to both our magazine and website secure and to only release this information to third parties we believe share our commitment to privacy.

According to the Attorneys General, such representations amounted to an unfair or deceptive act because Ziff-Davis did not take reason-

---

35. For more information on reporting incidents to law enforcement, *see* ch. 6.
36. *See* http://www.oag.state.ny.us/press/2002/aug/aug28a_02_attach.pdf.
37. *In re* Ziff-Davis Media Inc., *available at* http://www.oag.state.ny.us/press/2002/aug/aug28a_02_attach.pdf.
38. *Id.*
39. *Id.*

able precautions to protect the personal information of consumers ordering the *Electronic Gaming Monthly*.

The assurance of discontinuance agreement requires Ziff-Davis generally, among other things, to identify risks relating to the privacy, security, and integrity of consumer data, and to address those risks by means that include management oversight and training of personnel, monitoring of systems, and "establishment of procedures to prevent and respond to attack, intrusion, unauthorized access, and other system failures. . . ."[40] Unlike the settlement agreements reached by the FTC in *Eli Lilly* and *Microsoft* discussed previously, however, the assurance of discontinuance agreement reached by the Attorneys General and Ziff-Davis provides additional guidance on what constitutes reasonable security practices. Specifically, the agreement requires Ziff-Davis to, for example:

   (i) encrypt the transmission of consumers' sensitive data;
  (ii) detect unauthorized and suspicious activity regarding consumer data by enabling and monitoring automated tools such as server-logging and intrusion detection systems;
 (iii) implement authentication procedures to control local and remote access to consumer data;
 (iv) store consumer data in a database format that cannot be meaningfully interpreted if opened as a flat, plain-text file;
  (v) provide access only to authorized users by storing consumer data in a location inaccessible via http and/or protected by a firewall;
 (vi) review applications prior to implementation;
 (vii) implement risk identification and response controls; and
(viii) establish management oversight and employee training programs.[41]

Notably, in the agreement, the Attorneys General implicitly acknowledge the difficulty in determining what constitutes "reasonable security practices" by *not* requiring Ziff-Davis to undertake measures that are above and beyond what is generally accepted in industry. Ziff-

---

40. *Id.*
41. *Id.*

Davis is required to implement standard security practices only "where such standards have gained sufficient industry acceptance and adoption such that Ziff-Davis' adherence to the standards would not unreasonably place Ziff-Davis at a competitive disadvantage."[42]

II. Non-Regulatory Sources of Security Obligations

A. OPERATING RULES

Although statutory and regulatory requirements impose security obligations, security requirements can also arise from industrywide, network, and consortium rules. These rules can be binding through contracts or a network of contracts. Members might need to sign such contracts as a condition of participating in a particular industry group, network, or consortium.

For instance, the National Automated Clearing House Association (NACHA) oversees America's largest electronic payments network for the distribution and settlement of electronic credits and debits among financial institutions. NACHA develops and maintains the NACHA Operating Rules, which are enforced through contracts among financial institutions and other participants in automated clearinghouse transactions.[43] In 2001, an amendment to the NACHA Operating Rules permitted a new type of payment permitting online merchants to initiate a debit entry against a Web shopper's bank account after obtaining the consumer's authorization online.[44] As a condition of initiating debit transactions, the NACHA Operating Rules require these online merchants to employ stringent network and physical security requirements to protect consumers' financial information.[45]

Other organizations impose security requirements on their members through operating rules. For instance, credit card associations, such as VISA and MasterCard, require merchants and financial institutions to maintain certain levels of network and physical security.[46]

---

42. *Id.*

43. NACHA, Risk Management for the New Generation of ACH Payments iii (2001).

44. *Id.* at 21.

45. *Id.* at 34.

46. The VISA U.S.A. Cardholder Information Security Program, for example, defines a standard of care based on 12 basic security requirements for protecting cardholder information. *See* http://www.usa.visa.com/business/merchants/cisp_index.html.

Another example is the Identrus, LLC organization, a community of financial institutions that abide by certain operating rules and policies to support authentication for secure business-to-business electronic commerce. These rules and policies impose security requirements on the participants within the Identrus organization.[47]

B. AN ATTORNEY'S OBLIGATION TO SECURE ATTORNEY-CLIENT COMMUNICATIONS

While a majority of states express concern regarding e-mail exchanges between lawyers and their clients that contain confidential information, they do not require encryption of such e-mails. The American Bar Association Ethics Committee has endorsed that rule.[48] Because, the opinion states, there is a reasonable expectation of privacy in the use of unencrypted e-mail, except in the case of "highly sensitive matters," encryption is unnecessary. It does, however, require a lawyer to consult with the client "as to whether another mode of transmission, such as special messenger delivery, is warranted" when "the lawyer reasonably believes that confidential client information being transmitted is so highly sensitive that extraordinary measures to protect the transmission are warranted."

Nonetheless, recent advances in technology have made e-mail encryption more accessible. With the decreasing cost and burden of encryption and the increasing ease with which communications can be compromised, the standard of care may rise sometime in the future. Thus, if the legal profession unduly delays its adoption of new and available devices capable of avoiding—for a trivial cost—the risk of interception of clients' confidential information, lawyers may be held responsible for the breach of confidence, either as an ethics violation or for malpractice.

---

47. *See* Indentrus.com Knowledge Center Index (visited June 13, 2002), *available at* http://www.identrus.com/knowledge/index.xml.
48. ABA Standing Committee on Ethics and Professional Responsibility, Protecting the Confidentiality of Unencrypted E-Mail (Formal Op. No. 99-413 (1999)), *available at* www.abanet.org/cpr/fo99-413.html; *see also* Stein & Maslowski, *Attorney-Client E-Mail Puts Privilege and Confidentiality on the Line*, 4 THE INTERNET NEWSLETTER 1 (July 1999).

CHAPTER ❖ 4

Information Security Liability

This section discusses the statutory and common-law claims that can be asserted against people who launch or fail to prevent information security attacks. The government or victims of information security attacks may use these claims against the attackers or people who (intentionally or inadvertently) contributed to an attack. This section also discusses how organizations that fail to provide reasonable levels of information security can be subject to penalties or liable to those who are injured by their lack of adequate security. Section I summarizes some of the criminal statutes that apply to information security attacks. Section II discusses some of the civil claims that a victim of an information security attack can assert against the attacker or others. Victims of information security attacks may assert these same claims against organizations that fail to provide an adequate level of information security.

I. Cybercrime Laws

A number of laws have been enacted at the federal level that permit the prosecution of people and organizations that attack information systems. At least one law permits the victim to obtain restitution from the convicted attackers,[1] although restitution depends on whether the attacker has resources to pay the victims. Organizations should also be

---

1. 18 § U.S.C. 1030(g).

aware that if they have employees who attack information systems of others as agents of the organization, the organization itself can be held liable for criminal conduct. The principal criminal laws that apply to information security crimes are:

- *The Computer Fraud and Abuse Act*[2] (CFAA). This law covers computer fraud, intrusions, and related activity. The act applies to "protected computers." The term "protected computers" includes computers used by a financial institution or the United States Government, and computers that are used in interstate or foreign commerce or communications, which is construed to include any computer connected to the Internet. Under the Act, it is a crime to, among other things: (i) access a protected computer without authorization and knowingly and intentionally commit fraud; (ii) transmit programs and information that cause damage to a protected computer or access a protected computer without authorization and cause damage; and (iii) traffic in passwords in order to gain unauthorized access to protected computers. The jurisdictional limit based on a damage threshold for this statute is $5,000.[3]
- *The Electronic Communications Privacy Act of 1986* (ECPA).[4] ECPA prohibits unlawful access to, and certain disclosures of, electronic communications, including stored communications, and requires law enforcement to follow proper procedure in accessing electronic communications from third-party providers. The term "electronic communications" is defined as "any transfer of signs, signals, writing, images, sounds, data, or intelligence of any nature transmitted in whole or in part by a wire, radio, electromagnetic, photo electronic, or photo optical system that affects interstate or foreign commerce."[5]

---

2. 18 U.S.C. § 1030.
3. Companies should also be aware that employees' unauthorized access of third-party computers, if done while the employee is acting as an agent of the employer, may subject the organization to CFAA liability.
4. 18 U.S.C. §§ 2510-2521, 2701-2710. The Stored Communications Act, *id.* §§ 2701-2710, added the protections for stored communications.
5. 18 U.S.C. § 2510.

- *USA PATRIOT Act.* The Uniting and Strengthening America by Providing Appropriate Tools Required to Intercept and Obstruct Terrorism Act (USA PATRIOT)[6] was enacted to provide the government additional tools to assist in tracking, preventing, and combating terrorism in the wake of the September 11, 2001, attacks on the World Trade Center and the Pentagon. USA PATRIOT amends several preexisting laws, including the CFAA and the ECPA, discussed above, and broadly amends other areas of the law to achieve these objectives, including immigration laws, money laundering, jurisdictional matters, and the legal use of electronic surveillance by government sources. Although USA PATRIOT does not create specific security obligations for organizations, organizations should keep current, thorough, and accurate records of computer activity in order to assist the government in prosecuting intruders of computer systems and respond to government requests. In addition, the USA PATRIOT Act expands the scope of the Bank Secrecy Act, which requires covered institutions to develop and implement an anti-money-laundering program. Whereas before the enactment of this law only financial institutions were required to have such programs, the amendment extends these requirements to several other types of industries, including law firms if they engage in certain types of covered activities (most notably real estate closings and settlements). The Act requires the U.S. Treasury Secretary to establish regulations to carry out the requirements of section 326 of the Act, which provides that each covered entity must develop and implement reasonable procedures for (1) verifying the identity of any person (including non-U.S. persons) who wish to open an account; (2) maintain the copies of the records used to verify the person's name, address, and any other identifying information; and (3) determine if the person is on any list provided to the institution of known or suspected terrorists or terrorist organizations.
- *Homeland Security Act.* Section 201 of the Homeland Security Act assigns the newly created Department of Homeland Secu-

---

6. Pub. L. No. 107-56, 115 Stat. 272 (Oct. 26, 2001).

rity with responsibility over information analysis and infrastructure protection, which includes: (1) receiving and analyzing law enforcement information and intelligence; (2) assessing vulnerabilities of key resources and critical infrastructures; (3) integrating intelligence analyses and vulnerability assessments to identify and prioritize protective measures; (4) developing a comprehensive national plan for securing key resources and critical infrastructures; (5) taking the necessary measures to protect those key resources and infrastructures; (6) providing security and public threat advisories, and warnings to state and local governments and the private sector, as well as advice about appropriate protective actions and countermeasures; and (7) reviewing and recommending improvements to policies and procedures for sharing domestic security intelligence among and with federal, state, and local governments.

- *Access device fraud statutes.* The federal criminal code prohibits access device fraud,[7] which generally applies to the intentional misuse of credit and debit cards, passwords, and (therefore arguably) other authentication tokens.

- *Laws imposing privacy and security requirements.* Some of the laws described in Chapter 3, such as HIPAA, impose criminal penalties when a person intentionally violates an aspect of the law.

- *Criminal statutes addressing intellectual property infringement.* People who attack information systems in order to infringe on the intellectual property rights of others can be subject to criminal penalties. These acts may be punishable as a criminal violation of copyright rights (17 U.S.C. § 506(a); 18 U.S.C. § 2319), trademark rights (18 U.S.C. § 2320), and trade secrets (18 U.S.C. §§ 1831-1832). Also, the No Electronic Theft Act[8] creates criminal copyright liability even if the defendant does not obtain a financial benefit from the infringement, such as where a defendant hosts a Web site allowing for the free distribution of pirated software. Finally, the Digital Millennium Copyright Act[9] imposes criminal liability on persons seeking,

---

7. 18 U.S.C. § 1029.
8. 17 U.S.C. § 2319(c).
9. 17 U.S.C. § 1201.

for financial gain, to circumvent technologies used to protect intellectual property rights.

■ *Other federal statutes.* Other statutes that may impose criminal liability on attackers include those addressing harassment,[10] child pornography,[11] wire fraud,[12] and threats to injure the person or property of another.[13]

■ *State laws.* Many states have adopted laws prohibiting various forms of computer crime.[14]

II. Civil Actions

This subsection discusses some of the causes of action that a victim of an information security attack might assert against a party that had a duty to prevent but failed to prevent such an attack.[15] Such actions, if enough people are affected, could be consolidated into class-action litigation against the parties responsible for failure to stop the breach.

There has been a significant amount of speculation of the role tort or statutory liability may play in security compromises, although, as of the time of this writing, there have been no reported cases in the United States. There is at least one case, however, that took a first step toward addressing the damages caused by a company's lack of adequate security.[16] Other cases have been filed, but have not yet resulted in reported decisions.[17]

---

10. 47 U.S.C. §§ 223(a)(1)(C), (E).
11. 18 U.S.C. § 2252A.
12. 18 U.S.C. § 1343.
13. 18 U.S.C. § 875(c), (d).
14. *E.g.*, MINN. STAT. §§ 609.88, 609.89, 609.891; N.Y. PENAL LAW §§ 156.05, 156.10, 156.20-27, 156.30, 190.75-76, 250.00; UTAH CODE § 76-6-703.
15. Although a civil action could be commenced against the attacker, there are at least two reasons why such an approach might not make sense. First, the attacker is usually difficult, if not impossible, to track down. Second, the attacker (to the extent he or she can be found) will likely be subject to the criminal statutes.
16. C.I. Host v. DEVX.com Inc., 2002 U.S. Dist. LEXIS 3576 (N.D. Tex. 2002).
17. E.g., Stollenwerk v. Tri-West Healthcare Alliance, No. CIV. 03 0185 (D. Ariz., filed Jan. 28, 2003); Hamilton v. Microsoft (Cal. Super. Ct. L.A. County, filed Sept. 30, 2003).

A. CONTRACT CLAIMS

Information technology contracts, such as service agreements, software licensing agreements, or hardware purchase orders, are beginning to contain provisions imposing security obligations on vendors and business partners. Agreements increasingly require information technology providers to warrant against security vulnerabilities, such as viruses, worms, Trojan horses, logic bombs, and other similar mechanisms. Moreover, an organization may be contractually obligated to protect a customer's, employee's, or business partner's personal or confidential information.[18] Provisions addressing confidentiality often include a requirement to provide commercially reasonable protection of confidential information. Where such a term is a part of the contract, a party whose information is compromised may assert a claim against the party agreeing to provide security of the information under this provision.

These provisions are appearing in contracts between purchasers and technology vendors. For example, organizations might contract with companies that provide security-related products and services, or products or services with a security component. These can include companies that perform vulnerability assessments and penetration tests, antivirus software companies, outsourced managed security service providers, firewall vendors, network monitoring services, and operating system software companies. In contracts entered into between purchasers and vendors, the service providers might be subject to many, some, or no security requirements or warranties that the product/service conforms to a particular standard, depending on what the parties negotiate. Contractual liability can result from a breach of whatever standard is agreed to between the parties.

One broad class of technology vendors consists of the software manufacturers. Some vendors' software license agreements impose no requirements to prevent security breaches and attacks that exploit a

---

18. For instance, a HIPAA-covered entity may disclose individually identifiable health information to a business associate performing tasks on its behalf only if the HIPAA-covered entity obtains satisfactory assurance that the business associate will appropriately safeguard the information. 45 C.F.R. §§ 164.308(b)(1), 164.502(e)(1)(i). The business associate thus becomes bound to security obligations by contract.

vendor's products or services. In some cases, vendors may undertake to fix unknown security flaws in their products if and when such flaws are identified by customers. Other vendors shift more responsibility to the user, for example, by the forced use of security patches, mandating acceptance of fixes, and restrictive end-user agreements. While some software companies address the security issue upfront in an agreement, others may release products with known vulnerabilities, which increases the likelihood that a hacker/intruder will be able to compromise the product. It is important to note that the above discussion concerns commercial contracts; consumer agreements, because of consumers' relatively weak bargaining power, are more likely to omit vendor security requirements.

In addition to technology vendors, the victim of an information security compromise may assert a claim against customers, business partners and associates, and others (provided that a contractual relationship exists between the parties) if the victim's personal information resides on such entities' databases (or other means of storage) and is compromised. Unauthorized disclosure may result from a number of human causes, including a hacker's unauthorized access to the system, an inadvertent action by one employee, or a malicious employee action. Furthermore, unauthorized disclosure could occur as a result of flawed technology or improper implementation. Legal action against the entity for unauthorized disclosure is typically brought as a privacy class action and often stems from security breaches.[19] Unauthorized disclosure can also stem from breaches of nondisclosure agreements or confidentiality provisions within other types of contracts.

Statements in an organization's privacy policy can give rise to contractual liability if the organization fails to live up to its policy. A consumer may provide the organization with personal information in order to obtain a product or service. The organization's privacy policy may state that the organization will not disclose such information without the consumer's consent and/or will use some level of security measures to protect the information. If the policy is construed to be part of the agreement between the organization and the consumer and the organization fails to use adequate security measures, resulting in data

---

19. *See*, *e.g.*, Smith v. Chase Manhattan Bank USA, 9531B (N.Y. Super. Ct. 2002).

being lost, stolen or otherwise damaged, or if the organization intentionally or inadvertently discloses the information without the consumer's consent, the organization could be subject to contract liability if the consumer suffers any measurable harm.

B. NEGLIGENCE CLAIMS

Negligence is defined as the "failure to use such care as a reasonably prudent and careful person would use under similar circumstances."[20] For a plaintiff to win a negligence claim, four elements must be established:

- *Duty*. The defendant must have a legal duty of care toward the plaintiff.
- *Breach of duty*. The defendant must have violated a legal duty of care toward the plaintiff by a failure to act "reasonably."
- *Damage*. The plaintiff must have suffered harm.
- *Proximate cause*. The breach of the duty must be related to the plaintiff's injury closely enough to be considered the cause of, or at least a substantial factor in causing, the harm and must occur in an unbroken sequence from the injury.[21]

With respect to system or information compromise, there are several situations in which negligence liability could arise. One example is "downstream liability." Downstream liability refers to the liability an organization may face as a result of the tortious actions of an unrelated party. For example, in launching a distributed denial of service attack, the hacker first compromises the systems of several intermediary companies and uses those systems to launch the attack on the ultimate victim, resulting in a disruption of the victim's systems due to network overload. The victim may be able to assert a negligence claim against the intermediary companies, claiming that if those companies had used reasonable care in securing their systems, the hacker would not have been able to launch the attack against the victim.

Another scenario is where a hacker gains access to an organization's database and obtains names, addresses, and Social Security numbers

---

20. Black's Law Dictionary, 6th ed., 1032.
21. *Id.* at 1225.

that the hacker then uses to commit identity theft. The individuals whose private information was misappropriated may be able to assert a negligence claim against the organization, contending that in failing to use industry standard security measures such as firewalls or an intrusion-detection system, the organization failed to protect the victims' personal information and thereby proximately caused their damages.

Possible limitations to a successful negligence claim may include:

- *Uncertainty over whether a duty exists.* Existing law is not clear on whether a duty exists in the case of information security breaches when the parties do not have a preexisting relationship, whether contractual or otherwise. Several analogies in other types of tort cases, such as the landlord/tenant relationship, have been proposed.[22]
- *Uncertainty over "reasonable care."* There is considerable uncertainty over what constitutes "reasonable care" with respect to computer security due to the fact that: (i) security needs of organizations vary widely, and (ii) security technologies and industry standards are nascent and evolving. In addition, although prevailing industry practices will have some effect on the standard of care, they will not dictate its content in a court of law.[23]
- *Economic loss doctrine.* Under the economic loss doctrine, courts have barred recovery in tort for purely economic harm (i.e., financial loss) as opposed to physical harm or damage to property in an action based on negligence.[24] Since victims of information security compromises typically experience finan-

---

22. *See* Kimberly Kiefer & Randy V. Sabett, *Expert Report: Openness of Internet Creates Potential for Corporate Information Security Liability*, BNA ELECTRONIC COMMERCE AND LAW REPORT, Vol. 7, No. 24, at 594 (June 12, 2002).
23. Texas & P.R. v. Behymer, 189 U.S. 468, 470 (1903) (Justice Holmes's opinion, stating "[w]hat usually is done may be evidence of what ought to be done, but what ought to be done is fixed by a standard of reasonable prudence, whether it usually is complied with or not.").
24. Bilich v. Barnett, 103 Cal. App. 2d 921, 924 (1951). According to Black's Law Dictionary, economic loss is "a monetary loss such as lost wages or lost profits" and does not include personal injury or property damage. *See* Black's Law Dictionary 530 (7th ed. 1999).

cial loss in contrast to physical damage to computers, the economic loss doctrine could present a hurdle to successful information security claims. Victims, however, may be able to successfully recharacterize the loss as property damage to their computer systems, as has been done successfully in cases involving spam and data gathering.[25] In addition, some states appear willing to recognize exceptions to the economic loss rule in certain circumstances.[26]

C. STATUTORY CLAIMS

Victims of information security attacks may assert three kinds of statutory claims against their attackers. First, some of the cybercrime provisions discussed in Section I above create civil remedies for parties injured by criminal activities.[27] The victim of an information security attack can assert a claim against the attacker based on one or more of these statutes.

Second, the victim of an information security attack involving infringement on the victim's intellectual property rights can bring an action based on the misappropriation of such rights. For instance, attacks conducted to pirate software or other media create copyright liability.[28] Spoofing or impersonation may give rise to Lanham Act claims for trademark or service mark infringement. Moreover, espionage and other attacks to steal trade secrets may give rise to trade secret liability.

---

25. Erin Kenneally, *The Byte Stops Here: Duty and Liability for Negligent Internet Security*, 16 COMPUTER SECURITY J. (2000) at 20.
26. *See* J'Aire v. Gregory, 24 Cal. 3d 799, 804 (1979) (exception to economic loss rule where "special relationship" exists).
27. *E.g.*, EF Cultural Travel BV v. Explorica, Inc., 274 F.3d 577 (1st Cir. 2001) (Computer Fraud and Abuse Act); Konop v. Hawaiian Airlines, Inc., 2001 WL 13232 (9th Cir. 2001) (Electronic Communications Privacy Act and Stored Communications Act).
28. An example of an ongoing international copyright piracy investigation and prosecution undertaken by federal law enforcement is "Operation Buccaneer." This investigation has led to the sentencing of 13 defendants to federal prison terms of up to 46 months, which are the longest sentences ever imposed in the United States for Internet copyright piracy. *See* http://www.cybercrime.gov/ob/OBMain.htm.

Third, the victim may have claims under statutes prohibiting unfair competition and unfair business practices.[29] Such laws may also give victims causes of action against businesses whose failure to secure their systems contributed to their harm. These claims therefore may provide a claim in a downstream liability scenario, in addition to whatever other claims the plaintiff asserts.

D. SHAREHOLDER ACTIONS

Corporate directors and officers have a fiduciary duty of care to protect corporate assets. Since an estimated 80 percent of corporate assets today are digital,[30] oversight of information security falls within the duty owed by officers and directors in conducting the operations of a corporation. Generally, two rules govern the duty of directors and officers. The majority of cases follow the business judgment rule that the standard of care is that which a reasonably prudent director of a similar corporation would have used. Other jurisdictions have adopted a higher standard of care requiring the diligence, care, and skill that would be exercised by a prudent person in similar circumstances in his own personal business. To date, no shareholder suit has been brought against officers or directors for failure to take necessary steps to protect corporate systems and data; however, shareholders may have a valid basis for such derivative suits.[31]

In *Caremark International Inc. Derivative Litigation,* a Delaware court noted that officer/director liability can arise in two contexts: (1) from losses arising out of ill-advised or negligent board decisions (which are broadly protected by the business judgment rule as long as the decision resulted from a process that was rational or employed in a good-faith effort), and (2) from situations in which the board failed to act in circumstances where "due attention" would have prevented the loss. In the latter situation, the *Caremark* court noted that:

> [I]t would, in my opinion, be a mistake to conclude that . . . corporate boards may satisfy their obligation to be reason-

---

29. *E.g.,* Cal. Bus. & Prof. Code § 17,200 *et seq.*
30. *Cybercrime,* Business Week, Feb. 21, 2000.
31. Jody R. Westby, *Protection of Trade Secrets and Confidential Information: How to Guard Against Security Breaches and Economic Espionage,* Intellectual Property Counselor 4-5 (Jan. 2000).

ably informed concerning the corporation, without assuring themselves that information and reporting systems exist in the organization that are reasonably designed to provide to senior management and to the board itself timely, accurate information sufficient to allow management and the board, each within its scope, to reach informed judgments concerning both the corporation's compliance with law and its business performance. . . .

Obviously the level of detail that is appropriate for such an information system is a question of business judgment. . . . But it is important that the board exercise a good faith judgment that the corporation's information and reporting system is in concept and design adequate to assure the board that appropriate information will come to its attention in a timely manner as a matter of ordinary operations, so that it may satisfy its responsibility. [32]

The *Caremark* case could provide a basis for a shareholder suit against officers and directors for failure to implement an information and reporting system on the security of corporate networks and data. Liability could arise if they fail (1) to determine that the company is adequately meeting statutory, regulatory, or contractual obligations to protect certain data from theft, disclosure or inappropriate use, and (2) to be assured that the data critical to normal business operations, share price, and market share are protected.[33]

There are also high-risk situations where higher standards apply to directors and officers, such as acquisitions, takeovers, responses

---

32. Caremark International Inc. Derivative Litigation, 698 A.2d 959 (Del. Ch. 1996).

33. *See, e.g., id.*; for a general discussion on corporate liability related to board and officer responsibilities to ensure adequate information and control systems are in place, *see* Steven G. Schulman & U. Seth Ottensoser, *Duties and Liabilities of Outside Directors to Ensure That Adequate Information and Control Systems Are in Place – A Study in Delaware Law and The Private Securities Litigation Reform Act of 1995*, Professional Liability Underwriting Society, 2002 D&O Symposium, Feb. 6-7, 2002, *available at* http://www.plusweb.org/Events/Do/materials/2002/Source/Duties%20and%20Liabilities.pdf.

to shareholder suits, and distribution of assets to shareholders in preference over creditors. In these circumstances, directors and officers are required to obtain professional assistance or perform adequate analyses to mitigate the risks that ordinarily accompany these activities. Some information assurance experts assert that a "higher degree of care will also be required of Directors and Officers regarding the complex nature of issues involved in information assurance."[34]

Securities laws and regulations require public corporations to make adequate disclosures, in public filings and public communications, of relevant risks to the corporation and its assets. The *Independent Director* put this in the context of information systems by reporting that:

> Management of information risk is central to the success of any organization operating today. For Directors, this means that Board performance is increasingly being judged by how well their company measures up to internationally accepted codes and guidelines on preferred Information Assurance practice.[35]

Additionally, when a company is a victim of an attack on its information systems, whether from an insider or an outside attacker, studies have shown that the attack can result in a lack of confidence in the company and even a drop in the company stock price.[36] Consequently, shareholders may also initiate a derivative suit for loss to stock price or market share caused by inadequate attention by officers and directors to information security.

---

34. Dr. John H. Nugent, CPA, *Corporate Officer and Director Information Assurance (IA) Liability Issues: A Layman's Perspective*, Dec. 15, 2002, *available at* http://gsmweb.udallas.edu/info_assurance.

35. *Id.* (citing Dr. Andrew Rathmell, chairman of the Information Assurance Advisory Council, *Information Assurance: Protecting your Key Asset*, *available at* http://www.iaac.ac.uk).

36. A. Marshall Acuff, Jr., *Information Security Impacting Securities Valuations: Information Technology and the Internet Changing the Face of Business*, Salomon Smith Barney 3-4 (2000), *available at* http://www.ciao.gov/industry/SummitLibrary/InformationSecurityImpactingSecurities Valuations.pdf.

Clearly, these legal resources indicate that directors and officers need to undertake a certain level of involvement and oversight in ensuring that the organization is properly secured from an information security breach in order to protect against shareholder derivative suits.

CHAPTER ❖ 5

Information Security Best Practices

This section provides the reader with an explanation of some of the security management practices, controls, and safeguards that are prominent among industry-recognized lists of "best practices." Appendix B, to be read in conjunction with this section, provides examples of these practices. The statements in this section and Appendix B as to what an organization "should" do are recommendations only, and are based on what have been considered good security practices. They are not based on any stronger views of an organization's obligations, such as equating "should" with legal obligations. The reader would be wise to consult a professional in this area and exercise judgment to determine whether these practices are appropriate in light of an organization's particular situation.

This section and Appendix B are not a definitive or comprehensive listing of best practices and do not provide all of the technical details involved with security controls. It is not possible to build a definitive list of best practices, because security needs differ from industry to industry and organization to organization and because security technology changes rapidly. Therefore, this section's and Appendix B's purpose is simply to provide the reader with a high-level understanding of basic security practices. For references to other information, the reader should consult the list of standards, guidelines, best practices, and the resources contained in Appendix A.

I. Security Management Practices

Organizations holding sensitive information should ensure that basic security management practices are in place to create a climate conducive to handling specific security problems as they arise. Organizations should avoid the mistake of focusing mainly on technology solutions for information security challenges without spending enough time integrating the proper procedures, processes, and policies with technology solutions. Technology does play a key role in information security, but there is no "off the shelf" solution to information security challenges. Without policies, procedures, training, and operational guidelines, an organization will find it difficult to create an information security program to achieve its goals.

II. Authentication

Authentication is one of the principal challenges to securing information systems. The Internet makes authentication a significant challenge, since it creates a largely anonymous environment in which parties may not be certain with whom they are transacting. In an online environment, the identity of transacting parties cannot be ascertained by photo identification, signature comparison, or other identification methods typically available in a face-to-face setting.[1] The lack of authentication may lead to fraudulent or mistaken transactions.

Authentication is the process of ensuring that a person is who he or she claims to be. The authentication process can have two components, depending on the need for rigor in the authentication process. First, an authentication process includes ensuring that the person or name given in a transaction corresponds to a real-world identity. For instance, if a person attempts to open an account in the name of Jane Smith, authentication procedures can determine whether there is, in fact, a real Jane Smith with a certain identity. This authentication process provides assurances that the transacting party is not using a fictitious identity.

---

1. Of course, an online session could involve the transmission of scanned credential, video, or audio, but these data are subject to manipulation or to capturing and replaying them. Consequently, they are not the equivalent of a face-to-face meeting in which someone can compare a real person to an identification credential.

Second, assuming that a real-world identity exists, the authentication process can ensure that the person attempting to enter into the transaction does, in fact, correspond to the real-world identity. In our example here, authentication would attempt to confirm that an account application in the name of Jane Smith was, in fact, submitted by the real Jane Smith as opposed to someone attempting to impersonate Jane Smith. This portion of the authentication process provides assurances against the impersonation of a real person, such as in cases of identity theft. For a list of basic authentication practices, see Appendix B.

III. Physical Security and Physical Access Controls

An organization should carefully choose a location for its information systems to ensure adequate protection against physical intrusion, events that may damage the facility, and losses or disruption to important utilities and services. The layout of the building should also permit the control of access to specific zones so that only authorized personnel have access to those zones. The construction design of high-security zones should provide for materials (e.g., locks, doors, walls) of sufficient strength to deter and prevent intrusion. For a list of basic physical security practices and physical access controls, see Appendix B.

IV. Personnel Controls

An organization should implement controls to ensure that it is hiring competent, trustworthy employees. The organization should have a procedure to investigate applicants to ensure that a job candidate has qualifications that are appropriate for the position and the qualifications are as claimed by the candidate. Once the employee is hired, he or she should be given training and retraining to ensure continued competence. Personnel controls should also minimize the possibility of corruption by limiting access of the employee to areas that are necessary to the job function. In addition, employees should be restricted in their access so that the potential impact on the organization of a single malicious employee is minimized. Special termination procedures should be in place for employees leaving the organization. Finally, organizations should have procedures for the supervision of visitors and contractors and other persons temporarily on the premises to minimize their access to the physical plant, systems, and information. For a list of basic personnel controls, see Appendix B.

V. Network and Computer Security

Network and computer security threats are perhaps the most visible and publicized information security threats. Appendix B provides a basic list of security practices that mitigate the risk of network and computer security breaches.

VI. The Role of Lawyers

Lawyers play a crucial role in assisting an organization in implementing information security policies and practices. Their responsibilities include the following:

- Acting as a liaison between the corporate directors and managers, who hold the fiduciary duty for the organization assets, and the security specialists, who seek to protect those assets;
- Providing guidance in the drafting and implementing of the company's information security policies and ensuring compliance with those policies;
- Participating as an essential member of the incident response team for any internal or external security issues, including any legal requirement to advise law enforcement;
- Advising on product design from a legal perspective, with an eye toward ensuring compliance with security requirements;
- Advising on public relations matters and risk mitigation in the event of a compromise;
- Understanding and developing compliance strategies for security obligations resulting from applicable statutes;
- Providing guidance and counsel on the relevant laws;
- Monitoring developments in the law addressing negligence and other forms of liability in order to advise the organization about the current standard of care;
- Drafting agreements with third-party vendors to delineate responsibilities for ensuring security and managing the risks relating to information security; and
- Providing advice on ways to minimize contractual and other potential liability that may result from security breaches.

To fulfill these responsibilities, counsel must develop an understanding of the technologies employed by clients to protect their information assets, as well as the business and legal considerations involved in designing and implementing an information security program. Contact between the lawyer and the IT staff is crucial to achieve the appropriate balance of security, risk, and business productivity.

CHAPTER ❖ 6

Responding to Security Incidents

Total security is not possible. Despite the completeness and effectiveness of an organization's information security program, security breaches may occur. Just as important as an organization's ability to secure its systems is its ability to respond to a compromise. Effective response involves many steps, including: (i) development of an incident response policy; (ii) creation of an emergency response team; (iii) the ability to quickly and accurately determine what type of incident is occurring or has occurred; (iv) knowing when to involve other parties, including law enforcement; and (v) knowing who to contact in the case of an incident that may involve criminal activity.

Incident response policies should generally: (i) identify the incident response team; (ii) describe which events or actions require notification or disclosure to company management; (iii) describe which events or actions should be reported to law enforcement and the method of reporting such incidents; and (iv) identify which incidents may require forensic response and outside counsel and consultants.[1]

Incident response teams are also known as CIRTs (Computer Incident Response Teams) or CERTs (Computer Emergency Response

---

1. Marc J. Zwillinger, *Cybercrime: Developing a Computer Policy Framework: What Every General Counsel Should Know*, THE INTERNET NEWSLETTER, June 2001. *See also* CIO Cyberthreat Response & Reporting Guidelines, *available at* http://www.cio.com/research/security/incident_response.pdf.

Teams).[2] CIRTs usually involve company employees authorized to act in the case of an emergency, including management personnel, technical staff, legal counsel, and communications experts.

Determining whether a particular action or event is an incident can be challenging. Whereas "events" are typically any observable occurrence in a system and/or network (e.g., system boot sequence, system crash, packet flooding), an "incident" is an adverse event affecting the information system or the threat of the occurrence of such an event. CERT/CC offers a useful document for determining if your computer system has been subject to a security incident.[3]

When responding to an attack, initially the company must decide whether to focus on remediation (i.e., preventing further damage to systems) and/or investigation (i.e., preserving evidence in order to track down the attacker). Companies should strive to both remediate and investigate processes which, contrary to popular belief, often compliment and enhance each other. Organizations should contact law enforcement if the incident appears to involve criminal activity, indicated by any of the following events:

- An unauthorized user has logged onto the system;
- Abnormal processes are running on the system, using an abnormal amount of resources;
- A virus, worm, or other malicious code has infected the system;
- A user from a remote site is trying to access the system through atypical means of access, such as through a high-numbered port;
- A heavy volume of packets has bombarded the system in a short period of time (from the same or varied sources);
- There has been a compromise of root access;
- There has been an incidence of social engineering;
- There has been continuous network scanning or probing;
- The Web site has been defaced defaced or other data damaged;
- The attack appears to be aimed at critical information or areas of the network affecting critical infrastructure; or
- Data appears to have been obtained without, or in excess of, authority; or

---

2. "CERT" is the registered trademark of Carnegie-Mellon University. The CERT at Carnegie-Mellon is referred to as CERT/CC.
3. *See* http://www.cert.org/tech_tips/intruder_detection_checklist.html.

■ A denial of service attack has impaired the availability of data or the network itself.

As a general matter, in determining what to report to law enforcement, companies should report incidents that have a real and substantial impact on the organization or activity that is noteworthy or unusual, but should not report "routine probes, port scans or other common events."[4]

Once your organization has decided to contact law enforcement, it must decide whom to contact. The Department of Justice's Computer Crime and Intellectual Property Section has compiled a useful table that lists the type of crime and the corresponding appropriate federal investigative law enforcement agencies.[5] In addition, *CIO* magazine, in conjunction with the U.S. Secret Service (USSS) and the FBI, has issued "response and reporting guidelines" that list federal law enforcement agencies and their areas of responsibility, along with local FBI and USSS offices to contact in the event of an information security attack or breach.[6] As a general rule, for most types of computer intrusion, organizations should contact the local FBI office.[7] In recent years, law enforcement has established many groups that specialize in computer and intellectual property crime to respond quickly to security compromises, including, for example, one or more Computer and Telecommunications Coordinators in each U.S. Attorney's Office, 13 Computer Hacking and Intellectual Property Units, FBI Computer Crime Squads, and the United States Secret Service's Electronic Crimes Branch.[8]

Security incidents often are not reported to law enforcement agencies. According to the 2002 CSI/FBI survey,[9] only 34 percent of respondents who experienced computer intrusions reported those intrusions to law enforcement. While there are various rationales for this reluctance to report, the net effect seriously undermines general deterrence of computer crime, which leaves all networks much less

---

4. CIO Cyberthreat Response & Reporting Guidelines, *available at* http://www.cio.com/research/security/incident_response.pdf.
5. *Available at* http://www.cybercrime.gov/reporting.htm.
6. *See supra* note 4.
7. *See* http://www.fbi.gov/contact/fo/fo.htm.
8. *See* http://www.cybercrime.gov/enforcement.html.
9. *See supra* ch. 1, note 2.

secure. Even more salient: catching the hacker (and his computer) is frequently the only sure way to diagnose and end the problem.

Companies, further, may be required to report the incident to law regulators, enforcement agencies, or prosecutors. Regulated companies should check with their regulator to determine if they have a duty to report incidents and to whom they should report. Any duty under regulations will be industry-specific. For example, while a financial institution does not have a duty to report a security intrusion to its financial regulator, it is required to complete a Suspicious Activity Report (SAR) and file the signed form with the Financial Crimes Enforcement Network (FinCEN), which, sooner or later, will send the form back to the regulator. For a financial institution, notifying the regulator by sending a copy of the SAR is a best practice. Some states also have laws that have a reporting requirement.[10] Companies may even be required by law to disclose the fact of the security breach to customers. California, for example, enacted a statute, effective July 2003, requiring any state agency or person or organization that conducts business in California that owns or licenses computerized data to disclose to all customers who are California residents any breach of security of their unencrypted personal information.[11] In any event, a company that is required to report the event to any entity should certainly also report it to law enforcement.

In addition, some cyber insurance policies require the insured to report security incidents to law enforcement before a claim can be paid under the policy. Therefore, if the insured desires the loss to be covered under the policy, the incident must be reported. For these companies, not reporting to law enforcement is not an option.

There are a few simple rules for catching a hacker that companies should keep in mind:

1. Report immediately—delay kills.
2. Preserve evidence—copy logs.
3. Be quiet! Do not tell anyone who does not absolutely need to know. You can tell everyone after the hacker has been identified.

---

10. *See, e.g.*, MINN. STAT. § 609.8911; UTAH CODE ANN. § 76-6-705 (1993).
11. CAL. CIV. CODE §§ 1798.29, 1798.82.

CHAPTER ❖ 7

The Need for Risk Management

As mentioned in Chapter 1, one aspect of information security is the process that includes identifying the universe of possible threats to information assets, determining whether the information assets are vulnerable to these threats, and implementing appropriate and cost-effective safeguards to address them. Determining the threats to information assets and the degree of vulnerability is the process of risk analysis. The risk management process includes the risk analysis process and also includes the process of minimizing, accepting, or transferring risk through insurance and/or contracts.

In the private sector, it is important to consider information security risks as Board of Directors governance issues, as described in Chapter 4. Despite best efforts, security is a business risk that requires an ongoing risk management effort involving analysis, prevention, mitigation, and transference (if appropriate). Particularly with disclosure requirements facing publicly traded companies and regulatory oversight in certain industries, such as financial services and health care, these risks assume an ever-increasing profile among enterprise risk as a whole.

Other sections of this book focus on specific areas related to risk management. Chapter 2 provides information on the universe of information security threats. Chapter 1 discusses the need for organizations to conduct a risk analysis process by determining the degree to which an organization is vulnerable to threats. Chapter 5 summarizes various security practices, controls, and technology solutions that enable organizations to minimize risks, which are listed in more detail in Appendix B.

It is the responsibility of legal counsel, risk management, internal audit, and information security professionals to advise management of both the actual and potential costs involved with a course of action. Examining each step in the risk-management process not only prepares a company for potential losses, it also helps decision makers decide whether to take the proposed course of action. A proposed project can look attractive and profitable in the absence of risk. The safeguards and risk management process may add substantial costs to any information technology project, but building information security controls after the fact may prove more costly. A decision to adhere strictly to risk management practices and their associated safeguards is ultimately a business decision requiring consideration of both the costs and the ultimate value to the organization of the proposed action. In private-sector organizations, that analysis often involves return on investment (ROI) calculations.

The subsections of this section provide focused advice on three risk management topics. First, in determining whether to use a safeguard to minimize a risk, an organization must consider two factors: total cost of ownership (TCO) and its ROI. Section I describes TCO and ROI considerations that organizations should take into account in their risk management process. Second, Section II discusses considerations involved with accepting risk. It distinguishes between self-insurance and simply accepting a risk. Finally, insurance and contracts are a means of shifting risk. Section III discusses risk transfer issues relating to information security.

I. Total Cost of Ownership and Return on Investment Issues

No useful computer system is completely secure. Running a business necessitates taking risk. It is the job of a risk management team, composed of senior IT security, legal, audit, and insurance professionals, to assess accurately what risks exist, how to mitigate those risks, and what residual risks remain. Ultimately this risk assessment and mitigation strategy must be evaluated in light of the total cost of ownership and return on investment of security practices and safeguards. Clearly, a security plan that costs more to implement and maintain than the organization has in available revenue is not an option. Also, a security plan that does not reduce major security threats is not effective either.

Despite the constant drumbeat of the necessity of security precautions, the appropriate strategy is largely dependent upon the nature of an organization. While financial services and health-care organizations are respectively statutorily bound by GLB and HIPAA to a certain level of security that cannot be waived, many other organizations have much more flexibility. Moreover, many organizations that utilize the Internet only for promotional purposes could argue that firewalls, security monitoring services, and full-time security staff are unnecessary. Nonetheless, the implementation of some level of security practices is important to all organizations. On the plus side, information security can increase customer confidence and improve profitability. It is the basis of preventing significant losses or damage from a financial, brand, and operations perspective.

The TCO of information security solutions is often an elusive figure. While figures for the purchase and installation of various security products are easily quantifiable, there are many more subtle costs that must be considered.

Information security requires a focus on people, processes, and technology. It is the responsibility of every person employed by or having a relationship with the organization. Accounting for this participation makes calculating costs difficult. For example, the time it takes for an employee to remember and type his or her username and password and to log on and off each time he or she leaves the computer is a cost to the organization in the form of lost productivity. Such costs often are hidden at the time of implementation but are inevitably captured in the organization's bottom line. By clearly identifying these staff costs before proceeding with a security plan, managers can more wisely apply appropriate safeguards for an organization's financial capabilities and risk profile and thereby avoid costly surprises.

The ROI of security solutions is likewise difficult to quantify. The principal ROI for an organization adopting a security solution is the *absence* of a loss or damage. What would the damage have been had the organization not adopted the solution? It is impossible to know for certain because the solution avoided the loss or damage. Some security solutions provide capabilities, marketing advantages, and resulting increased business and revenue. These aspects of ROI are easier to calculate. However, the main loss-avoidance return is difficult to quantify.

Nonetheless, the absence of an absolutely certain ROI does not justify an organization abandoning its efforts to secure its information systems. People have an intuitive notion that minimizing risk and liability has a financial value. It is for this reason that people purchase automobile insurance policies beyond what the law requires, even though the ROI of insurance is also difficult to quantify.[1]

The better practice is for an organization to conduct a reasoned analysis of risk and the benefits of loss prevention, mitigation, and transference from a qualitative as well as quantitative perspective. Information security loss analysis must recognize the negative impact on brand or customer trust, exposure to litigation or regulatory enforcement, disruption of operations, and loss or disclosure of highly valuable confidential information. Preventing these events should also be given considerable weight in determining the benefits of adopting a safeguard.

II. Self-Insurance and Risk Assumption

No business decision is without risk. By making use of state-of-the-art security models and technologies, companies have been able to reduce costs, improve the quality of products and services, and increase profits. Even after all cost-effective safeguards are in place, however, residual risks remain. The organization must continue its business notwithstanding the remaining risks. Many organizations undertake substantial information security risks based on the knowledge that such risks will be dwarfed by the value produced by the proposed course of action.

If an organization does not use insurance or contracts to shift risk to a third party (an insurance company or vendor), that organization will have to plan for the potential impact of these residual risks on its financial statement.

The notions of risk acceptance and self-insurance embody two distinct concepts. The first is active self-insurance, by which an organization, while accepting the residual risk, seeks to be prepared for

---

1. Presentation by Dr. Herbert Lin, ABA Annual Meeting (Aug. 9, 2002).

such an eventuality by setting aside funds to cover the potential loss and liability or by creating a "captive" insurance carrier subsidiary that insures the parent's risks. The notion of active self-insurance assumes that the enterprise has allocated funds to meet these risks. All organizations self-insure to some extent. However, companies that choose this option should consider its tax implications. It may be difficult to write off the cost of maintaining that reserve fund as a business expense. Captive insurance may address this issue, but this option can be complicated.[2]

The other type is passive self-insurance, often known simply as acceptance of a risk. When an organization accepts risks passively, it does not set aside funds and must pay the damages for a realized risk using whatever resources are available at the time. Again, all organizations are required to face some risks that they have neither the insurance nor the financial reserves to cover. For many organizations, this is the risk taken when operating a business. There will always be unavoidable risks that threaten to bankrupt the organization. To prevent this, most companies purchase insurance for the larger, unpredictable, or catastrophic risks and passively self-insure smaller, manageable risks. While risks always exist, their severity and unpredictability must be significantly reduced for an organization to instill confidence in its stakeholders.[3] In some cases, investors could bring a cause of action against the directors and officers who did not prudently prevent and control the impact of large, unexpected self-insured losses.[4]

Insurance policies do not cover all possible losses and liabilities that an organization may sustain. The deductible or self-insured retention is the risk the organization assumes. Self-insured retention means that the organization pays the loss and/or expenses up to the retention amount, before the insurance carrier has the financial obligation. However, in its non-capitalized form, it more closely describes the passive form of self-insurance described above.

---

2. *See* Marc M. Harris, *The Need for Captive Insurance, available at* http://www.cyberhaven.com/offshorelibrary/captive.html; *Captives, available at* http://www.mimsintl.com/content.asp?cid=188.
3. *See generally Information Security Risk Assessment: Practices of Leading Organizations, at* http://www.gao.gov/special.pubs/ai00033.pdf.
4. *See generally supra* ch. 4, § II.D.

Both active and passive measures have their role in an organization's risk management program. The extent of the use of both will depend on the circumstances of the threats and vulnerabilities, the importance of the information or information systems at stake, and the cost and effectiveness of safeguards. Where a particular threat poses a remote chance of insignificant harm, and the cost of safeguards and active self-insurance is high, then passive measures may be appropriate. As the risk increases, active measures may become more cost-effective.

III. Insurance

Insurance provides a means by which an organization can shift or transfer residual risk to a carrier that, for the price of the premium, agrees to take on that risk. Another method of transferring risk is through contracts with vendors or other parties.

There are a number of issues associated with transferring information security risks through contracts. Technology vendors that provide Internet or computer network–related services typically limit their exposure and exclude all consequential damages. Further, an indemnification provided by a vendor that is not backed by assets and/or insurance has limited value. Based upon the security risk posed by vendors and their services, companies should consider requiring their vendors to purchase network security insurance, which is part of cyber insurance product (discussed below), to protect themselves from vendor-caused security breaches or outages.

The other method of transferring risk is through insurance. Traditional insurance policies (such as property insurance, commercial general liability, and crime) were not designed around networked computers, electronic information, and the Internet. Property policies only respond to the physical destruction of tangible property, including computer equipment, from events like fires or windstorms. Commercial general liability policies address bodily injury and tangible property damage to third parties, typically liability arising out of business premises or products. They do not address damage or loss associated with data security.

Many of the most significant cyber risks are either not covered or not covered adequately by traditional insurance. Disputes could arise with these insurers over the interpretation of insuring agreements, definitions, and exclusions. In today's insurance market, traditional insurers may eliminate previously granted coverage upon renewal, such as direct and indirect losses arising out of computer viruses. Court decisions may reinterpret policy language to further affect future coverage. Importantly, cyber risk policies are separate from business liability policies. Those organizations that have not purchased cyber liability coverage should be aware that their existing business liability coverage is likely to be construed to exclude damages resulting from information systems.[5] Also, these policies may list certain events that are not covered. Therefore, a careful review of the policy by the insurance buyer or risk management professional, attorney, and insurance broker is essential.

As a result, organizations need to look to the cyber risk insurance products, which were released starting in 1999 and are increasingly becoming available to organizations. The transition toward using insurance to protect against information security threats, however, has not been a smooth one.

The insurance business is based on determining the probability of a risk being realized and then spreading out the cost of that impact over a large population of insureds in the same risk category. That practice has worked relatively well for hazards that have been known for decades. Recently emerging hazards to information resources present difficulties for insurance companies because they lack the actuarial data sufficient to determine the probability that certain risks will be realized. These difficulties became apparent after September 11, 2001, when many insurance companies either dropped or significantly increased the price of terrorism insurance until the Terrorism Risk Insurance Act was enacted in November 2002. Information security poses similar difficulties. Because information technology is relatively new and networked systems are in their infancy, both the probability of a risk being realized and the magnitude of the risk are not known.

---

5. *See* America Online, Inc. v. St. Paul Mercury Ins. Co., Civ. Action No. 01-1636-A, 207 F. Supp. 2d 459 (E.D. Va. 2002) (insurer had no duty to defend under comprehensive general liability insurance policy covering "property damage" because software, data, and systems are not "tangible property").

Insurance providers tend to offer new types of coverage for one of two reasons. First, they may offer coverage because the number of customers demanding a certain type of coverage reaches critical mass. Second, they may offer coverage because the market for existing types of insurance policies is slow, and providers perceive an opportunity in offering a new type of coverage. Some insurance providers have moved toward offering a new type of policy, generally called a cyber risk policy or a network security liability policy. These policies are specifically designed to address the risk to a business that arises from operating Web sites and computer networks. Some insurance carriers provide coverage for both first-party (direct) loss and liability losses; others provide coverage for only third-party losses.

A limited number of providers currently offer cyber risk policies, such as AIG, CNA, Lloyd's of London, and Zurich. Organizations seeking to cover their residual risk, after increasing awareness and protecting their organization as well as practicable, should investigate cyber liability coverage.[6]

---

6. Neither the ABA nor the authors recommend a particular policy or issuer. There are a number of Web sites that contain a description of these products, such as www.chubb.com and www.aignetadvantage.com.

CHAPTER ❖ 8

Conclusion

Information security is a challenge for organizations. The struggle against terrorism reminds us that we must be on our guard against future attacks. The next major attacks may indeed arrive through cyberspace. The stakes for protecting information have never been higher, because of the great emphasis in our economy on information as a source of value and wealth. The purpose of this book is to provide the reader with basic information about security threats, laws creating compliance issues for organizations, and possible criminal and civil claims that impose liability for information security breaches, as well as high-level guidance concerning good information security and risk management practices.

While an organization cannot achieve total information security, the high stakes involved underscore the need to invest in information security. The alternative is unacceptable: loss of critical information, cost and expense in recovering from an attack, liability, and even, possibly, the demise of the organization itself. There is no quick fix or "security off the shelf," because information security practices must be tailored for an individual organization and continually reevaluated as assets and business processes change. With this book, the ISC seeks to raise awareness of the importance of information security, spread knowledge of the issues, and provide a resource for finding more detailed information as the need arises.

APPENDIX ❖ A

Standards, Guidelines, Best Practices, and Other Resources

I. Standards for Enterprise Security

- International Organization for Standardization, *ISO/IEC IS 17799:2000* (under revision) provides a framework for developing and implementing a comprehensive security program. ISO 17799 comprises a set of controls for best practices in information security that is divided into 10 sections: business continuity planning, system access control, system development and maintenance, physical and environmental security, compliance, personnel security, security organization, computer and network management, asset control and classification, and security policy.
- International Organization for Standardization, *ISO/IEC TR 13335, Guidelines for the Management of Information Technology Security (1996-2000)* (under revision).
- Information Security Forum, *Standard of Good Practice*. This standard provides a statement of good practice for information security from which businesses can measure their performance. The standard is targeted at large international organizations.
- Information Systems and Audit Control Foundation, *Control Objectives for Information and Related Technology* (COBIT).

COBIT's objective is to develop and promote an international set of generally accepted information technology (IT) control objectives for day-to-day use by business managers as well as security, control, and audit practitioners. COBIT has been developed as a generally applicable and accepted standard for good IT security and control practices that provides a reference framework for management, users, and information systems audit, control, and security practitioners.

II. Standards for Software Development and Operational Benchmarks

- The Center for Internet Security (CIS) has developed "security configuration specifications that represent a prudent level of due care." It has developed security benchmarks for technical security configurations across a wide range of operating system platforms and Internet software applications. **www. cisecurity.org**
- The SANS Institute, *SANS "Score"*: Community of security professionals working to develop minimum standards and best practices, essentially acting as the research arm for CIS. **www. sans.org**
- Software Engineering Institute, *Capability Maturity Model* (CMM). **www.sei.cmu.edu/cmm/cmm.html**

III. Standards for Systems Security

- National Security Agency, *Security Recommendation Guides*. NSA has developed and distributed configuration guidance for several different platforms, including Microsoft Windows 2000 and NT. These guides are currently being used throughout the government and by numerous entities as a security baseline for their systems. In addition, the Router Security Configuration Guide provides technical guidance and is intended to help network administrators and security officers improve the security of their networks. **http://nsa2.www.conxion.com/**
- American Institute of Certified Public Accountants and Canadian Institute of Chartered Accountants, *SYSTRUST Principles and Criteria for Systems Reliability*. Review process for sys-

tems reliability – security, availability, integrity, maintainability.

- National Institute of Standards and Technology, *Generally Accepted Principles and Practices for Securing Information Technology Systems.* **http://csrc.nist.gov**
- International Organization for Standardization, *Common Criteria for Information Technology Security Evaluation (ISO/IEC IS 15408: 1999).* The Common Criteria is a process or language through which product and security evaluation standards can be written, and then a particular product, component, or system evaluated.

IV. Standards for Products Security

- National Institute of Standards and Technology, *Federal Information Processing Standards (FIPS)* 140-2 Standard for Cryptographic Systems.
- *Common Criteria,* III *supra.*
- *Open Source Security Testing Methodology Manual.* The Manual sets forth a standard for Internet security testing.
- *BITS Tested Mark product certification.* **www.bitsinfo.org/sloverview.html**

V. Best Practices and Guidelines in Information Security

- ABA Section of Science and Technology Law, Information Security Committee, *Digital Signature Guidelines* (1996).
- ABA Section of Science and Technology Law, Information Security Committee, *DKI Assessment Guidelines* (2003).
- Business Software Alliance, *Are You Cyber Secure?* **www.bsa.org/security**
- Organisation for Economic Co-Operation and Development, *Guidelines for the Security of Information Systems and Networks.* The OECD has recently revised its 1992 Guidelines for the Security of Information Systems. The Guidelines set forth high-level principles that are essential to developing a culture of information security. **www.ftc.gov/bcp/conline/edcams/infosecurity/popups/OECD_guidelines.pdf**

- National Institute of Standards and Technology, *An Introduction to Computer Security: NIST Handbook, 1996.* The Handbook provides a comprehensive approach to security planning and security program development and implementation, starting from a risk management framework.
- National Institute of Standards and Technology, *NIST Risk Management Guide for Information Technology Systems.* NIST Special Publication 800-30, 2001.
- Visa International Inc., *Account Information Security Standards Manual.*
- Visa International Inc., *Visa Best Practices for E-Merchants.* In order to reduce the risk of online credit card fraud, Visa requires merchants that accept Visa cards online as a form of payment to follow a set of "best practices."

VI. Standards for Disclosing Security Vulnerabilities

- Organization for Internet Safety

VII. Electronic Signature Standards

- 21 C.F.R. pt. 11 (standards for submission of electronic records to the FDA). **www.21cfrpart11.org.**
- HIPAA Electronic Signature Standard, 63 Fed. Reg. 43,242, 43,268-69 (proposed electronic signature standard, which has not been finalized).

APPENDIX ❖ B

Examples of Information Security Best Practices

I. Security Management Practices

- Security policies and procedures should be established that clearly outline the organization's security measures governing the protection of sensitive information, assets holding or processing that data, and access to them. Policies and procedures should involve not only the information technology staff, but also personnel from areas such as legal, risk management, internal auditing, marketing, office of the chief privacy officer, human resources, public relations, and internal auditing. A diverse team of people needs to be involved in the planning, development, and implementation of security policies and procedures.
- In drafting policies and procedures and implementing security safeguards, organizations should analyze risks and decide which to reduce through specific safeguards, which to transfer through insurance, and which to accept.
- Standards, guidelines, lists of best practices, and other resources may help an organization draft security policies. A list of such resources appears in Appendix A. One prominent example is the International Organization for Standardization's ISO 17799,

which provides a benchmark by which the security of all organizations can be measured.

■ Security policies should be consistent with applicable privacy requirements and the organization's privacy policies.

■ A "top-level" security policy sets the overall organizationwide security requirements and policies, and demonstrates commitment of the organization to information security. In addition, however, an organization may have many different types of security policies. Examples of such security policies are acceptable use, e-mail monitoring, document retention, disaster recovery, incident response and handling, authorization, access control, password, and authentication policies.

- *Acceptable Use Policy.* An acceptable use policy provides guidance to employees and supervisors of an organization by outlining what use of information systems is acceptable in the workplace. Subjects of the policy can include e-mail, voice-mail, and computer equipment provided by the company as well as conduct that will not be tolerated by the employer (e.g., it is unacceptable to access pornographic sites). A typical acceptable use policy will state that information systems provided by the company (i) should be used for business purposes; (ii) should not be used to harass, discriminate or defame other employees or individuals; (iii) should not be used to download or install unlicensed software; (iv) should not be accessed by people who are not authorized to use company equipment; and (v) should not be used to transmit confidential or proprietary information.

- *E-mail Monitoring Policy.* Although computer equipment and the electronic data generated by or stored on the company computer equipment is considered the property of the company, the federal wiretap statutes prohibit monitoring of wire and electronic communications unless an exception applies. Consequently, an employer may not monitor the use of the equipment, including e-mail, unless, for example, it does so to protect its assets or it obtains the consent of the individuals party to the communications.[1] If an organization has a business need to monitor e-mail, it should implement a policy telling employees, business partners, and others who use the organization's equipment that the organization monitors the use of and content on its computer equipment and use of the system constitutes consent to such monitoring.[2] Such policies, when summarized and placed on the computer prior to logon, are known as monitoring "banners."

■ *Document Retention Policy.* Increasingly, businesses are storing documents in digital format, and in many cases, digital format is the only format that is used. This trend is creating significant new challenges that make it compelling to adopt and implement a document retention policy (DRP). An effective DRP will address, among other issues, what documents need to be retained, how long must they be retained, how to show who created or signed a retained document, how to demonstrate whether a document has been altered over time, if changes to a document are permitted and a record is crucial, who made what changes to a document when, and how the organization can ensure its ability to access a document over a possibly long retention period.

■ Organizations should hire a staff of qualified security personnel that can implement and enforce the organization's security policies and practices. The security staff should be large enough to perform the tasks called for in such security policies and practices. In addition, depending on the size of the organization and requirements under law, the organization may want to establish a Chief Information Security Officer position that reports directly to a member of senior management.

---

1. 18 U.S.C. § 2511.
2. For more information, *see* Searching and Seizing Computers and Obtaining Electronic Evidence in Criminal Investigations, Computer Crime and Intellectual Property Section, Criminal Division, Department of Justice, July 2002, *available at* http://www.cybercrime.gov/s&smanual2002.htm.

- Directors, business managers, and executives should create a culture of security[3] by endorsing security policies and procedures, facilitating their implementation, and demonstrating management buy-in to employees.
- Security education and training are crucial for employees of the organization. Training should include procedures for periodic retraining and reminders. Organizations should also provide security awareness training to customers, contractors, vendors, business partners, and others who may have access to sensitive information or information systems of the organization.
- Organizations should develop procedures to report, handle, and respond to security incidents and compromises. Organizations should have the capability to take immediate action to identify an incident, contain any damage, and, if necessary, preserve evidence for possible actions against the person responsible for the incident.
- Organizations should develop, review, and test disaster recovery and business continuity plans periodically. Backup copies of information should be available on alternative equipment, offsite, or even at alternative operational sites so that business can continue despite the failure of one set of equipment, one site, or the main network. For instance, a redundant data center in the Midwest could serve as a "hot site" to allow continued operations if an earthquake were to destroy the main data center in California. Disaster recovery and business continuity plans should be broad enough to encompass any number of disasters that might befall the organization, ranging from natural disasters to denial-of-service attacks that disable the organization's Web site.
- Organizations should monitor compliance with their security policies and procedures to ensure that they are being implemented and enforced. Among other mechanisms, organizations holding sensitive information should undergo periodic security audits by qualified auditing professionals. It is helpful to

---

3. The concept of a "culture of security" has recently been addressed by the OECD Guidelines for the Security of Information Systems and Networks, *available at* http://www.ftc.gov/bcp/conline/edcams/infosecurity/popups/ OECD_guidelines.pdf.

base audit criteria on recognized standards, guidelines, and
best practices such as ISO 17799 and those listed in Exhibit A.
Results of the audit should be reported to the organization's
management, and any deficiencies in security should be rem-
edied promptly.

- If the organization outsources some information technology
or security functions, it should conduct a due diligence investigation to ensure that the provider is capable of performing
the outsourced functions and enforces robust security policies
and practices. The organization should carefully delineate responsibilities, risks, and liabilities borne by the organization
and the outsource provider in the contract. In addition, it should
monitor and supervise the provider's personnel and periodically assess and audit the provider's performance. The organization should have contingency plans in the event the provider
is no longer able to perform its obligations.

II. Authentication

- There is no one single "best practice" regarding the procedures for authenticating users to ensure that they correspond
to a real-world identity. Although authentication using at least
two authentication means (two-factor authentication) is considered to be the most secure alternative, several possible authentication procedures are possible. At the low end of the scale,
users may authenticate themselves using passwords they choose
themselves. Self-chosen passwords may not be secure, since
they may choose the names of their spouses or children, which
are easily guessed, or words in the dictionary, which automated
systems may be able to break with so-called "dictionary attacks." The use of passwords can be strengthened by enforcing certain rules, such as requiring passwords of a certain length,
using both numbers and letters, and using both upper- and
lower-case letters.[4]

---

4. Requiring the use of two different passwords at different points in the authentication or transactional process could also increase security. Nonetheless, the burden of having two different passwords for a single system may
not be acceptable to users.

- More complex authentication schemes may make use of tokens, such as cards or hardware devices. Cards with magnetic stripe information are tokens, although smart cards with chips and cryptographic keys are even more secure. Attackers would need to steal the token or be able to replicate the information on it to impersonate the token holder. Thus, requiring users to use a token to perform the transaction provides some assurance that the user is who he or she claims to be.

- Authentication systems can also make use of "biometric" methods of authenticating people. Biometric systems are based on some characteristic of a person's biological makeup, such as a fingerprint, iris pattern, or voice pattern. For instance, a fingerprint-reader system for authenticating users may require them to obtain a device that they can plug into a PC. When a user wants to authenticate herself prior to a transaction, she places her finger on the reader, which checks to determine if the pattern matches the user's stored pattern. If so, the user is authenticated and can proceed with the transaction.

- To increase security, authentication procedures can combine more than one of the factors described. The three potential factors of authentication are (1) something that you know (e.g., PIN or password), (2) something that you have (e.g., a token), and (3) something that you are (i.e., a biometric identifier). Using two-factor authentication (i.e., combining two of these three factors) increases the rigor of the authentication procedure. In theory, one could use all three factors for even greater security.

- Digital signatures supported by a public key infrastructure also serve to authenticate users. Digital signatures depend on public key infrastructures (PKI) of various kinds. Some PKIs use "digital certificates" as online credentials to support digital signatures. Other PKIs may use trusted databases of information instead of digital certificates. Still other PKIs are based on the use of various eXtensible Markup Language (XML)-based protocols[5] to supply the cryptographic keys needed to verify digital signatures.

---

5. These protocols are various XML signature specifications of the World Wide Web Consortium and the XML Key Management Specification (XKMS).

- One of the crucial steps in implementing any authentication system is to educate users about protecting password, PINs, tokens, shared secret cryptographic keys used to create digital signatures, and the like. Without such education, the possibility of security compromises of these authentication data may become the weak link in the system. To prevent this vulnerability, the organization implementing an authentication system can provide information to users about steps they can take to prevent the loss, theft, and unauthorized disclosure of these items and emphasize to the user the importance of protecting them.

- The choice of authentication procedures will involve a tradeoff between rigor of the process on one hand and, on the other hand, increased cost and difficulty of use. Many systems rely on simple user-chosen passwords because they are easier and less costly to administer than other methods. Nonetheless, organizations using these systems bear greater security risks than organizations using more rigorous procedures. The use of more rigorous procedures may, however, entail the cost and effort of obtaining, distributing, and supporting tokens or biometric readers. Consequently, organizations should balance the risks and benefits of various authentication methods before choosing one. The cost of the method chosen should be commensurate with the risks faced and the benefits provided.

- When a user creates a relationship or opens an account with an organization, the organization may want to take steps to ensure that the name in the application corresponds to a real-world identity and that the applicant is, in fact, the person named. A range of possible authentication procedures are possible. They include relying on databases of information kept internally or maintained by others. For instance, an authenticating organization can utilize systems based on credit report information in which applicants are asked a series of financial questions that presumably only the applicant would know in order to see if the answers match the information in the database. The rationale for such systems is that anyone answering questions with enough accuracy is likely to be the real person named in the application within reasonable tolerances. The information in databases may be more or less reliable, depending upon the way in which the information was compiled. It is generally considered more rigorous for an individual to appear in person before a representative of the authenticating organization to present identification credentials, such as a driver's license or passport. The representative can check the validity of the credential and ensure that the picture on the credential and the face of the person before him match. Such a step provides assurances of both the existence of a real-world identity and the fact that the applicant is the real person.

- Online merchants can authenticate themselves to consumers using Web server digital certificates and secure sockets layer (SSL) technology. The server certificate acts as a credential that authenticates the merchant's Web server. A certification authority asserts in a digital certificate that a cryptographic key (a public key) belongs to a certain organization, such as a merchant. An SSL session requires the server to prove possession of the private key corresponding to the public key in a certificate issued to the merchant. Moreover, the domain name in the certificate must match the domain name being accessed.

- In addition to choosing and implementing appropriate technologies and methods for authentication, effective authentication also requires documentation of authentication policies and practices. Documentation prevents breakdowns in security by ensuring that employees have clear, uniform procedures to follow. Documentation also evidences the due diligence performed in the authentication process in case there is a need to defend the authentication procedures in a lawsuit.

- An organization will not only want to authenticate its customers and other users, it will want to authenticate its own employees and contractors.

- Organizations should ensure that they authenticate personnel who will have to access sensitive information and critical systems. During the process of hiring an employee, companies and other organizations often confirm that the new employee has a real-world identity, and they keep records of that check (e.g., Social Security number and documents showing immigration status to fill out Immigration and Naturalization Service Form I-9). Organizations may want to leverage that opportunity to authenticate new hires for security as well as immigration status–checking purposes.

- Organizations can control access to systems and information using the authentication factors mentioned above for users, such as passwords, tokens, and biometric identifiers.

III. Physical Security and Physical Access Controls

- Critical network, server, and telecommunications equipment must be placed in physically secure locations that permit access only to authorized personnel.
- Data centers holding equipment and systems containing sensitive information should be protected by security guards, alarms, and cameras.
- Originators should use security badges and security badge readers to restrict access to authorized personnel. In the high-security zones, they should also consider the use of biometric access readers that permit access based on fingerprints, iris scans, facial recognition, or other biometric parameters.
- An employee's or other person's access to such equipment or areas where sensitive information is stored should be permitted only when necessary to that person's job function.
- Personnel should ensure that the sensitive information they work with on their desks, on computer screens, on shelves, or in drawers is not accessible to personnel not authorized to see it.
- Multi-person access controls should be implemented to ensure that it takes multiple persons to open successive doors, cabinets, and other barriers to access high-security zones. Such controls help to ensure that one person acting alone cannot circumvent established safeguards.
- Disaster recovery and business continuity plans should address natural and man-made disasters and security incidents affecting the organization's facility and physical resources.
- Proper environmental controls, such as ventilation systems, and reliable utilities, such as water and electricity, should be considered in facilities planning. Plans should include procedures or facilities in the event of disruption—for instance, having a

backup power generator to provide an alternative power source in case of a power blackout. Equipment to detect and handle hazards such as fires and floods are a critical part of the planning process as well.

- The organization should conduct an inventory of critical equipment (such as computer servers, workstations, and laptops) periodically and investigate any discrepancies uncovered by an inventory. Discrepancies may be an indication of theft.
- The organization should categorize its documentation and media (e.g., floppy disks and backup tapes), implement policies concerning the segregation and protection of sensitive documents and media, and ensure that they are shredded, erased, or destroyed after their useful life to protect against attackers searching garbage for sensitive information ("dumpster diving").

IV. Personnel Controls

- Hiring procedures should be established that, at a minimum, verify application information (including the identity of the applicant) and check references on new employees who will have access to sensitive information. In higher-security settings, background-checking procedures can include a check of other information, such as criminal records, other public records, and financial information. Organizations may wish to repeat background screening periodically or when an employee is being considered for a promotion. The idea of such screening procedures is to ensure that applicants for positions of trust do not have a track record of criminal activity or untrustworthiness.
- Employees should be properly and thoroughly educated on information security and the organization's policies and practices, as well as their job functions and individual responsibilities.
- Organizations should minimize employee access to sensitive information. Employees should have access to only the sensitive information that they have a need to know. The organization should provide them with the least amount and scope of

privileges (e.g., access to systems and information) needed for them to perform their job duties.

- Organizations should segregate duties, critical processes, and access control so that it takes multiple persons to access certain systems or information or to perform certain functions. These controls make it more difficult for a single individual to gain unauthorized access or to perform operations in an unauthorized fashion. Controls should also provide safeguards to prevent the circumvention of mechanisms enforcing segregation.

- Organizations should have a system of employee discipline to deter and redress security violations. Employees should be aware that security violations may result in sanctions that could include termination.

- Procedures should be established to ensure that terminated employees have no access to secure information or secure areas, and that they return all keys, access devices, and other tokens permitting access to physical locations or computer systems. Any user accounts and passwords for network access should be disabled. Organizations should also secure the return of critical property given to terminated employees, such as laptops.

- Visitors should be provided access to secure areas or information only when essential, and they should be accompanied by an employee at all times. Contractors and other temporary users should be supervised carefully by the organization's personnel in charge of managing them. They too should be given access only to information that they need to know to perform their assignments.

V. Network and Computer Security

- Information technology personnel should analyze the network used by an organization to ensure that the network's configuration is consistent with secure practices. Moreover, organizations should evaluate Web server uptime and capacity to ensure that transactions can take place without interruption and that capacity can keep up with anticipated demand. Personnel should also monitor and, where necessary, maintain logs of what software is being used on which equipment. Organizations should ensure that software is configured properly.

- Access to networks should be restricted to authorized and authenticated users through the use of passwords, logon codes, security tokens, biometric access devices, digital certificates, or a combination of these mechanisms. To ensure accountability, each user should have a unique account or set of access privileges. Employees should be warned about deceptive attempts to fool users into revealing passwords ("social engineering"), careless password handling (e.g., writing it on an adhesive note left near the user's workstation), and eavesdropping techniques, such as watching a user input his password ("shoulder surfing").

- Distribution of or access to sensitive information should be limited, with procedures and controls in place to govern its distribution and access, and the need for distribution of or access to such information should be reviewed, verified, and approved.

- The organization should obtain, install, and regularly update anti-virus software for its workstations and servers.

- From time to time, software vendors make available software fixes ("patches") intended to address security vulnerabilities. Organizations should monitor bulletins, publications, listservs, Web sites, and other news sources identifying new types of attacks and vulnerabilities in software that they use, obtain the patches produced by the vendor to fix the vulnerability, and apply them promptly to the extent feasible.

- Organizations should "harden" their operating systems, other software, and hardware using industry-recognized guidelines. For instance, organizations should remove or turn off unnecessary software services and applications, some of which may be turned on under default settings. The fewer the number of applications on a system, the easier it is to maintain its security.

- Procedures should be developed to move and store all sensitive information behind firewalls and in systems not accessible from the Internet. Sensitive information should not be stored on a Web server. Firewalls must be fully developed with se-

cured processes in place for administering them, and firewalls should protect Web sites from inappropriate and unauthorized access, as well as denial-of-service attacks.

- Organizations may need to take additional steps besides implementing a firewall to defend against denial-of-service attacks. For instance, they may find it helpful to utilize additional routers on network perimeters to filter packets entering networks. Organizations should also ensure that they have adequate Internet bandwidth and backup Internet connections in case an attack is launched through connections with the main Internet service provider. An organization should have incident response procedures in place to respond to attacks and work with its ISP to filter packets upstream from the organization's network.

- Organizations should make use of and maintain intrusion detection systems, network-monitoring software, and security assessment tools to detect attempts to penetrate the organization's networks. Organizations may either handle the monitoring process internally with a team of security practitioners or outsource the process to vendors that offer managed security services, which monitor various segments of the organization's infrastructure and handle some degree of incident response.

- Security incidents and significant events (e.g., major upgrades in software) should be logged to provide an audit trail for later investigation, prosecution, and auditing. Periodic review and analysis of system logs may detect security vulnerabilities.

- Sensitive information (i.e., account information, routing number, Social Security number, private identity and authentication data, etc.) should, to the extent possible, remain in encrypted form when transmitted across networks or stored. Encryption provides protection against unauthorized disclosure of information even if an organization's networks are penetrated.

- To minimize the vulnerability of sensitive information to unauthorized viewing or hacking by attackers and the potential for its theft or misuse, organizations should use a commercially reasonable security technology that provides a level of security that, at a minimum, is equivalent to 128-bit SSL encryption technology. SSL not only permits an organization to

authenticate itself to a user, it creates an encrypted channel between a user's workstation and an organization's Web server. At the time of this publication, 128-bit SSL encryption technology meets industry standards for the secure transmission of sensitive information. Technological advances, however, may alter what is reasonable encryption.

- Data retention schedules should be developed that detail policies on how to handle sensitive information from the time of capture to destruction, and reviews of such policies should be conducted to ensure that these retention schedules are being met.

- Data should not be retained for longer than necessary, and permanent storage of information should be considered only if required by applicable laws, regulations, or rules of a governing organization.

- Security systems, processes, and software should be regularly tested to ensure that they operate properly. Organizations should consider conducting periodic network penetration testing to determine whether their networks are vulnerable to attack.

- Network and computer security technologies are best used in combination pursuant to a strategy called "defense in depth," which means using more than one layer of defense in securing computer systems and networks to make penetration into such systems and networks more difficult.

- Disaster recovery and business continuity plans should include provisions to recover from attacks against an organization's systems or networks.